A Comprehensive Library Staff Training Programme in the Information Age

D0279973

CHANDOS
INFORMATION PROFESSIONAL SERIES

Series Editor: Ruth Rikowski
(email: Rikowskigr@aol.com)

Chandos' new series of books are aimed at the busy information professional. They have been specially commissioned to provide the reader with an authoritative view of current thinking. They are designed to provide easy-to-read and (most importantly) practical coverage of topics that are of interest to librarians and other information professionals. If you would like a full listing of current and forthcoming titles, please visit our web site **www.chandospublishing.com** or contact Hannah Grace-Williams on email info@chandospublishing.com or telephone number +44 (0) 1865 884447.

New authors: we are always pleased to receive ideas for new titles; if you would like to write a book for Chandos, please contact Dr Glyn Jones on email gjones@chandospublishing.com or telephone number +44 (0) 1865 884447.

Bulk orders: some organisations buy a number of copies of our books. If you are interested in doing this, we would be pleased to discuss a discount. Please contact Hannah Grace-Williams on email info@chandospublishing.com or telephone number +44 (0) 1865 884447.

A Comprehensive Library Staff Training Programme in the Information Age

AILEEN WOOD

Chandos Publishing

Oxford · England

020.7155
WOO

Chandos Publishing (Oxford) Limited
Chandos House
5 & 6 Steadys Lane
Stanton Harcourt
Oxford OX29 5RL
UK
Tel: +44 (0) 1865 884447 Fax: +44 (0) 1865 884448
Email: info@chandospublishing.com
www.chandospublishing.com

First published in Great Britain in 2007

ISBN:
978 1 84334 118 5 (paperback)
978 1 84334 119 2 (hardback)
1 84334 118 2 (paperback)
1 84334 119 0 (hardback)

© Aileen Wood, 2007

Typeset by Domex e-Data Pvt. Ltd.
Printed and bound in Great Britain by 4edge Ltd, Hockley. www.4edge.co.uk

Contents

List of figures and tables

Figures

Tables

Preface

This book is intended to be an introduction to staff training. Colleagues across the world were contacted to see what type of material should be included such a book, and it has consequently been developed from material used to train library and information professionals, such as workshops, courses, seminars and frameworks.

Chapter 1 starts by reviewing the competencies and skills required by library and information staff to carry out their work role or designated tasks effectively and efficiently. To ensure that their workforce stays fit for purpose and fit for practice, an organisation must have an effective training and development strategy to address any performance gaps or deficiencies in the workplace. The need to conduct a training needs analysis is discussed in Chapter 2.

Staff will have identified their own training needs through a number of sources, one of which is the performance appraisal (Chapter 3). From the appraisal, staff should have personal development plans to create a clear plan of action for an individual to complete over a given period of time. The plan will cover areas of learning, objectives or goal setting, as well as defining gaps in development. Chapter 4 explores the need to have an up-to-date curriculum vitae and gives some useful tips on how to prepare for an interview.

A key ingredient of the learning process is to understand how people learn and identify their preferred style of learning. Chapter 5 briefly outlines some key models of learning styles.

Library and information staff are increasingly devising and designing their own courses. Chapter 6 covers a systematic approach to planning a learning experience, administration, evaluation and equipment.

The knowledge, experience and expertise required of library and information staff is diverse and has developed beyond traditional librarianship skills. Chapter 7 provides some examples of training courses that have been run for those working in the information profession, together with expected learning outcomes. The selection indicates the progressive nature of the discipline.

Training and development activities may be undertaken using a range of methods and techniques. A selection of the more popular training methods and techniques is outlined. Chapter 8 on informal non-conventional training techniques concentrates on the importance of mentoring and coaching in the workplace.

To deliver training effectively, a person must be skilled in the art of facilitation. Chapter 9 reviews group dynamics and how to handle conflict, as well as giving other pointers on facilitating groups.

There are many learning opportunities where library and information professionals may acquire knowledge and update their skills. Chapter 10 emphasises the opportunities that are available through academic, professional and vocational training. Assessing prior learning acknowledges that a person already possesses many skills, knowledge and expertise, but these need to be balanced against the organisation's needs. The main assessment methods are listed. Many qualifications require an individual to submit a professional portfolio. This section gives some pointers on how to build a portfolio and write a reflective account. The framework of qualifications as used by the Chartered Institute of Library and Information Professionals (CILIP) in the UK is presented as an example of a professional scheme.

About the author

Aileen Wood has a professional background in training and development, records management, information science and special librarianship. She is self-employed but continues to work with the information profession, running training workshops and supporting staff completing professional qualifications. For her PhD she researched the need for a national health information policy. Aileen has written or co-authored a number of publications.

Aileen holds membership of several professional associations. She is a Fellow of the Chartered Institute of Library and Information Professional (CILIP). As an active member of CILIP, Aileen is a member of the Accreditation Board that reviews university LIS course curricula, and on the Assessment Panel for the Paraprofessional Certification Qualification. In 2006, Aileen was co-administrator on the local organising committee for the European Association for Health Information Librarians Conference 2007, in Cluj-Napoca, Romania.

Aileen has spent most of her working life in the public sector, having worked as the Legal Information Officer and Data Protection Officer for Surrey County Council and as Information Officer for the Ministry of Defence. In her previous employment she has worked as the Training and Information Services Officer at the Centre for Applied

Microbiology and Research; setting up the library services for the Football Association; as IT Officer at the Library Association; and was involved in the completion of the retrospective conversion of the Royal Military College of Science's library catalogue.

From 1996 until 2003, Aileen worked for the London Library and Information Development Unit as the Training and Development Coordinator. Her remit was to ensure the competency of the healthcare library and information services staff. She was responsible for the delivery of a progressive modular training programme and a range of staff development activities. Aileen spent a lot of time supporting staff on a one-to-one basis and making extensive visits to the service points around London, Essex and Hertfordshire.

The author may be contacted at the following address:

Dr Aileen Wood
13 Woolwich Close
Bursledon Green
Hampshire SO31 8GE
UK

E-mail: *govanwood@yahoo.co.uk*

LIS competencies and skills

Introduction

There are various definitions of competence and competencies. For the purpose of this chapter, the following description from the Special Libraries Association, will be used:

> Competencies are a combination of skills, knowledge, and behaviours important for organisational success, personal performance and career development. Professional competencies relate to the special librarian's knowledge in the areas of information resources, information access, technology, management and research, as well as the ability to use these areas of knowledge as a basis for providing library and information services. Personal competences represent a set of skills, attitudes and values that enable librarians to work efficiently, be good communicators, focus on continuing learning throughout their careers; demonstrate the value-added nature of their contributions; and survive in the new world of work. (Special Libraries Association, 1997: ix)

When gaining awareness, Weightman (1994: 67) suggests that competence moves through four key stages:

- *Appreciation*: Know what is meant by a term and what its purpose is.

- *Knowledge*: Understand in some detail the principles of the topic and how they are applied.

- *Experience*: Have acquired knowledge and skills.

- *Ability*: Be able to apply knowledge and skills with satisfactory results.

The conscious competency model (Figure 1.1) is used to explain the process and stages of learning a new skill (behaviour, technique or ability). The model originally had four phases, but a more recent version defines a fifth stage of competency awareness. The stages are as follows:

Figure 1.1   Conscious competence model

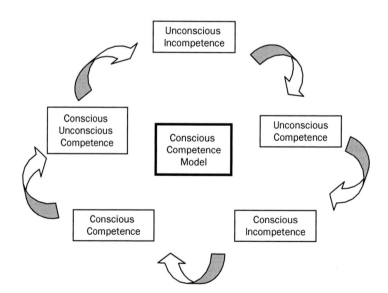

NB Ownership of the competency model has not been attributed as it is uncertain who originated the concept

LIS competencies and skills

Introduction

There are various definitions of competence and competencies. For the purpose of this chapter, the following description from the Special Libraries Association, will be used:

> Competencies are a combination of skills, knowledge, and behaviours important for organisational success, personal performance and career development. Professional competencies relate to the special librarian's knowledge in the areas of information resources, information access, technology, management and research, as well as the ability to use these areas of knowledge as a basis for providing library and information services. Personal competences represent a set of skills, attitudes and values that enable librarians to work efficiently, be good communicators, focus on continuing learning throughout their careers; demonstrate the value-added nature of their contributions; and survive in the new world of work. (Special Libraries Association, 1997: ix)

Competencies relate to the minimum level of performance expected of staff members to carry out their work role or designated tasks effectively and efficiently. They underline the behaviours necessary to achieve a desired outcome. These competencies may be acquired through programmes of education, training and other vocational learning or through experiential activities.

Competency awareness models

The individual functions at two interrelated levels, namely:

- *Personal*: Set of skills, attitudes and values (see Table 1.1).
- *Professional*: Expertise on area of subject knowledge, information resources and provision of service (see examples given below).

Table 1.1   Examples of skills and personal attributes and values helpful to information professionals

Professional values and attributes	
Adaptability	Honesty
Appreciating diversity	Intellectual curiosity
Commitment	Keenness to learn
Creativeness	Patience
Showing respect for individual	Persistence
Energy and enthusiasm	Positive outlook
Enterprising	Precision and accuracy
Enthusiasm	Responding to individual needs
Flexibility	Willingness
Good judgment	Willingness to take risks

| Table 1.1 | Examples of skills and personal attributes and values helpful to information professionals (*Cont'd*) |

Management and transferable skills	
Management and soft skills	Managing a service
Change management	Meetings and committee work
Client liaison/customer care	Negotiation skills
Coaching and mentoring	Performance appraisal
Communication and listening skills	Personal development plans
Decision making and problem solving	Project management
Employment and legal issues	Public relations
Finance and budgeting	Quality management
Interpersonal skills	Recruitment and selection
Interviewing	Report writing
Job evaluation	Strategic and business planning
Leadership	Team development and motivation
Managing a resource	Time management
Managing staff	Writing aims and objectives
Information communication and technologies skills	
Audiovisual	Library automation
Database construction	Networking
Data management	Office systems
Data input	Online communications
Data mining	Programming
Data restructuring	Retrospective conversion
Desktop publishing	Search engines
DOS	Software support
E-mail systems	Systems administration
Graphics	Systems analysis
HTML, Java scripts	Systems design
Internet/super highways	Video conferencing
Intranets	Webpage design
Keyboard skills	Windows environment

When gaining awareness, Weightman (1994: 67) suggests that competence moves through four key stages:

- *Appreciation*: Know what is meant by a term and what its purpose is.

- *Knowledge*: Understand in some detail the principles of the topic and how they are applied.

- *Experience*: Have acquired knowledge and skills.

- *Ability*: Be able to apply knowledge and skills with satisfactory results.

The conscious competency model (Figure 1.1) is used to explain the process and stages of learning a new skill (behaviour, technique or ability). The model originally had four phases, but a more recent version defines a fifth stage of competency awareness. The stages are as follows:

Figure 1.1   Conscious competence model

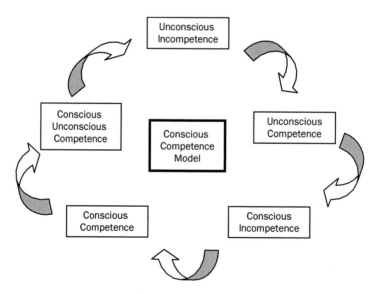

NB Ownership of the competency model has not been attributed as it is uncertain who originated the concept

- *Stage 1 – Unconscious incompetence*: Unaware of the skills required or that knowledge is lacking; below the standards required to carry out the task; unable to understand or answer user enquiries; sometimes in denial that there is a skills deficiency; the individual must be motivated to learn, and acknowledge that there is a reason to find out and appreciate the benefits to be gained.

- *Stage 2 – Conscious incompetence*: Uncomfortable, as the individual is aware of how poorly they are performing and mindful of learning needs; they are aware of how much there is to learn and the deficit skills yet to be addressed; they have a measured understanding of skills required to become competent.

- *Stage 3 – Conscious competence*: Gaining knowledge and experience but in need of further practice to gain mastery; starting to gain theoretical knowledge; beginning to understand concepts; conscious concentration is required to perform the task, but the individual is able to perform the task without seeking assistance.

- *Stage 4 – Unconscious competence*: Mastered the skills needed; at ease with what has to be done; the task becomes second nature; the individual can perform the task without the need to stop and think; theoretical knowledge has been transformed into practical knowledge; the individual is able to multi-task.

- *Stage 5 – Conscious unconscious competence*: Enlightened awareness of skills and abilities; the individual completes tasks instinctively; is able to help others and endow them with these skills; they have intuitive reactions gained from experience and are reflective and aware of the need to refresh skills.

To reach the final stage, the individual must progress through each level; it is not possible to skip a stage. Progression through the stage has been likened to an awakening experience. Some people may stop at stage 3 as this quite often equates with the minimum performance standard required by the organisation. At stages 4 and 5, it is possible for complacency to surface, whereby bad habits set in and the individual forgets to update skills, knowledge and competencies. In such a case, regression occurs, taking the individual back to a lower stage.

Corporate competencies

Corporate competencies look holistically at all the business skills needed for an organisation to function effectively. In the workplace, corporate competency is normally reviewed at five performance levels according to responsibility and seniority:

- *Director/chief executive*: Strategic and fiscal management of organisation, including political, tactical and diplomatic relations, e.g. corporate planning.

- *Senior management*: Management of department or sector, with a degree of autonomy, e.g. staffing, planning, budgeting.

- *Professional*: Management of team or project, deputising, some financial responsibility, professional work, e.g. cataloguing, information retrieval, research.

- *Para-professional*: Responsible for certain areas, supervision, e.g. day-to-day running of service, stock maintenance.

- *Non-professional*: Within remit of post, responsible to others for routine work, e.g. issues, overdues, shelf tidying, clerical.

In the workplace, competences tend to be used for two main functions: professional growth and development, and recruitment, retention or promotion purposes. These functions are intrinsically linked. On appointment, the crucial questions to be asked are 'What are the minimum requirements for this post?' and 'What does the post-holder need to be able to do to perform each task efficiently?' With training, 'What level of performance would be expected at the end of the training period?' and 'What level of performance would be expected when fully competent?'

Individuals must be able to correlate their role to the business function and the competencies required by the organisation to fulfil its role, for example, what is the business of the organisation, who are the clients and how do I fit into it? The individual needs to be able to articulate in language understood by the business staff and by the clients.

Absolute and tolerant competencies

Competencies may be described as absolute or tolerant. The former are normally linked to targets or timescales (e.g. all journals to be booked in by 10 a.m.), while the latter may have a tolerance rating (e.g. actioning 80 per cent of the interlibrary loans within 72 hours). It is also recognised that some competencies may be dependent on other people's actions (e.g. I cannot do my task unless you complete your task).

When writing competencies, it is important to get the right balance between over-generalisation and prescription. If the statement is too general, the competency will be vague and open to multiple interpretations. Where the competence is presented in minute detail, it becomes over-prescriptive and controlling. This has been likened to 'working to rule'. Some areas, however, will demand tightly controlled competences; these usually revolve around health, safety, security and legal issues.

Core and generic competencies

What competencies individuals require is dependent on the level of seniority, specialism and sector, whether part of a large organisation or in singleton posts (e.g. solo librarians). Certain areas may be defined as 'core competencies', these are the activities that set the library and information profession apart from other occupations.

Generic competencies apply to any group in any discipline and are usually referred to as 'transferable skills'. These competencies include a range of attitudes, values and skills from flexibility, valuing diversity, and technological skills, to interpersonal skills, strategic planning and resource management.

According to Boulter, Dalziel and Hill (1996), 'threshold' competencies are the characteristics that any jobholder needs to perform the job effectively to a satisfactory level. People whose performance excels beyond minimum competencies are seen to have 'differentiating' competences and are sometimes referred to as superior performers.

To operate effectively within the information environment, the LIS professional must be able to:

- Work within agreed codes of professional practice.

- Conform to the ethical standards of the profession.

- Exercise professional judgment and justify actions taken.

- Be professional at all times irrespective of status.

- Be an advocate for the library and information services.

The guidelines set out by the International Federation of Library Associations and Organisations (IFLA, 2000) recommend ten core curriculum elements:

1. The information environment, information policy and ethics and the history of the field.

2. Information generation, communication and use.

3. Assessing information needs and designing responsive services.

4. The information transfer process.

5. Organisation retrieval, preservation and conservation of information.

6. Research, analysis and interpretation of information.

7. Applications of information and communications technologies to library and information products and services.

8. Information resource management.

9. Management of information agencies.

10. Quantitative and qualitative evaluation of outcomes of information and library use.

Table 1.2 presents some core and generic competencies required by librarians in order to operate effectively within the information environment. The following descriptors apply to these competencies:

Table 1.2 Examples of LIS competencies at professional, paraprofessional and non-professional level

	Staff skill level		
Competence	Professional	Paraprofessional	Non-professional
Abstracting, indexing and thesaurus	Abstract and index material and construct a thesaurus	Locate and retrieve transcripts of abstracted items	Use a variety of indexes
Acquisitions and processing	Develop policies and procedures for selection, acquisition, circulation, maintenance and weeding of library materials	Identify the main sources for the acquisition of material	Process material ready for use
Archives administration	Implement the policies and procedure relating to the preservation, conservation and storage of archival documentation	Implement document control, procedures and record retention scheduling	Maintain accurate files and filing systems particularly relating to company documentation such as minute books and reports
Business management and development	Prepare and write the business plans, development strategies, project proposals, progress reports and funding bids	Implement the business plan	Support the business activities of the library

Table 1.2 Examples of LIS competencies at professional, paraprofessional and non-professional level (*Cont'd*)

	Staff skill level		
Competence	Professional	Paraprofessional	Non-professional
Cataloguing and classification	Apply the rules and regulation relating to cataloguing and classification of material	Create accurate records with appropriate codes	File and retrieve materials using the cataloguing and classification schemes
Change management	Anticipate internal and external changes, trends and influences that affect the development of the library services	Embrace change and accept new challenges, responsibilities, and assignments	Adapt to changing circumstances in the workplace
Collection development	Create and develop collection management policies in line with the overall purpose of the organisation	Engage in the maintenance and development of the different collections such as reference, loans, journals, audio, photographic	Maintain the integrity of shelf order and filing for each collection of material
Communications	Communicate with staff and users at all levels, demonstrating effective listening skills and actively seeking constructive feedback	Communicate using a variety of means – in person, in writing by telephone and by electronic means	Communicate with users and understand their needs

Table 1.2   Examples of LIS competencies at professional, paraprofessional and non-professional level (*Cont'd*)

Competence	Staff skill level		
	Professional	Paraprofessional	Non-professional
Current awareness and selective dissemination of information services	Provide current awareness services including the use of bulletins, web pages, newsletters and fact sheets for the dissemination of information	Provide tailor-made service by profiling user needs and through selective dissemination of information services	Respond to users' needs for current information
Desk and enquiry work	Devise and implement policies relating to user enquiries and user services	Assist users with their requests for information and answer complex enquiries	Issue, discharge and renew materials, action overdues and ensure that all records are up to date
Information evaluation and critical appraisal	Critically evaluate and assess existing and new information resources in relation to user needs	Understand the importance of providing accurate and timely information	Provide information in the correct format
Financial management	Plan, prepare, and manage all financial resources including budgets, funding streams and other sources of income ensuring compliance with legal and regulatory requirements	Assist with maintenance of financial records in accordance with local practices and procedures	Collect fines and handle other petty cash transactions e.g. buying photocopying card

Table 1.2 Examples of LIS competencies at professional, paraprofessional and non-professional level (*Cont'd*)

Competence	Staff skill level		
	Professional	Paraprofessional	Non-professional
Identification and analysis of information flows and resources	Review workflows and patterns and understand how they impact on information services	Liaise with customers/ clients about the direction of the service and identify trends	Assist with the collation of data on library trends and usage
Human resources	Demonstrate knowledge of relevant employment laws including equal opportunities, diversity and other human rights	Assist with the implementation of HR procedures in the workplace	Work within the terms and condition of employment
Information communications and technologies	Develop and implement strategies for ICT applications to manage the information resource including databases, integrated library systems, client-server applications, hardware, software, networks and electronic information systems	Maintain all systems to support housekeeping and information retrieval functions such as library catalogue and membership details	Demonstrate good keyboard skills and work in the Windows environment using a range of applications and packages

| **Table 1.2** | Examples of LIS competencies at professional, paraprofessional and non-professional level (*Cont'd*) |

Competence	Staff skill level		
	Professional	Paraprofessional	Non-professional
Interlibrary loans	Work in partnership with other agencies for resource sharing	Understand the procedures to obtain material from other sources, taking into account local practices, legal issues and other factors	Verify bibliographical details before submitting requests to other libraries
Information policy development	Devise, develop, implement and review a library and information strategy in line with organisational policies and procedures	Contribute to the development of a library information strategy	Understand the role of the library in the organisation
Knowledge management	Contribute to knowledge management strategy of the organisation	Gather, organise and share knowledge in terms of resources, documentation and people skills	Pass on information as part of a knowledge management gathering exercise
Languages	Liaise with users and colleagues at appropriate levels according to technical language or subject terminology	Arrange for the translation of material into and appropriate language or format as required by the user	Provide materials in appropriate format to suit user needs, e.g. Braille, large print, audio

Table 1.2	Examples of LIS competencies at professional, paraprofessional and non-professional level (*Cont'd*)

	Staff skill level		
Competence	Professional	Paraprofessional	Non-professional
Leadership and teamwork	Build strong work relationships with team members, colleagues, management, and users through effective leadership	Provide effective support to staff through a range of tasks and activities	Work effectively as part of a team and earn respect
Legal and regulatory issues	Work within the legal, regulatory and organisational frameworks relating to copyright, licensing, intellectual property, patents, service level agreements, freedom of information, data protection, transborder flow of information, and health and safety	Demonstrate a knowledge of legal and regulatory requirements that affect the provision of a library service	Demonstrate an understanding of the copyright, freedom of information and data protection laws
Manage a library service	Manage the library staff, resources, facilities and amenities including building, stock and capital expenditure	Work with appropriate agencies responsible for maintenance, repairs and improvements to the library service	Accept ownership and take responsibility for own actions

Table 1.2   Examples of LIS competencies at professional, paraprofessional and non-professional level (*Cont'd*)

Competence	Staff skill level		
	Professional	Paraprofessional	Non-professional
Marketing and public relations	Implement a marketing and public relations strategy to promote the importance of the library service to users, managers and other agents	Develop and provide marketing information products for use within and outside the library service	Provide information to users on library services
Organisational	Demonstrate and understand the social, political, cultural and economic context in which the organisation works	Work in a fluid environment within an organisational structure	Describe the organisation's core values and what they mean
Personal development	Demonstrate a commitment to lifelong learning, personal growth and professional career development for all library staff	Reflect critically on personal effectiveness and professional development	Engage in developmental activities
Planning and organisational skills	Ability to develop short, medium and long-term plans for the development of the service, ensuring these meet the requirements of the organisation and users	Assist with the implementation of service plans to advance the library services	Demonstrate an awareness of the short, medium and long-term plans for the library

Table 1.2 Examples of LIS competencies at professional, paraprofessional and non-professional level (*Cont'd*)

Competence	Staff skill level		
	Professional	Paraprofessional	Non-professional
Professional and ethical issues	Demonstrate a knowledge and commitment to the ethics and values of the profession and the organisation	Demonstrate an awareness of professional ethical issues relating to the delivery of the library services	Show awareness of ethical issues relating to the delivery of the library services
Principles of library and information science	Demonstrate an awareness of the processes and techniques whereby information resources are created, analysed, evaluated, moderated, manipulated and delivered in order to meet the requirements of a defined user population	Demonstrate an understanding of user needs and provide excellence in service	Demonstrate an understanding of the library's role, purpose and responsibility within the organisation
Problem solving and decision-making	Encourage others to make good decisions and take ownership in decision making and problem solving, by providing appropriate direction and assistance when necessary	Make decisions based on sound evidence and consider the implication of the outcome in the workplace	Take ownership and responsibility for own actions taken in the workplace

Table 1.2   Examples of LIS competencies at professional, paraprofessional and non-professional level (*Cont'd*)

	Staff skill level		
Competence	Professional	Paraprofessional	Non-professional
Project management	Describe and implement the principles of project management	Demonstrate a willingness to follow through on projects	Understand the importance of completing tasks and adherence to timescale
Research and critical evaluation	Identify key components and concepts in research topics	Undertake research into appropriate sources and databases, to obtain material and critically evaluate the information	Assist clients with research using both print and electronic resources
Searching	Construct complex searches and critically evaluate documents retrieved for authenticity and relevance to topic	Construct a search strategy and use a range of tools to interrogate relevant sources and databases to obtain the information	Retrieve information from electronic, print and multimedia formats
Service performance assessment	Appraise service and evaluate performance in line with organisational objectives	Work with service performance frameworks	Work with service performance frameworks

Table 1.2 Examples of LIS competencies at professional, paraprofessional and non-professional level (*Cont'd*)

	Staff skill level		
Competence	Professional	Paraprofessional	Non-professional
Staff performance assessment	Appraise and evaluate staff performance by giving constructive feedback and providing opportunities for staff development	Demonstrate a commitment to personal and professional development	Show commitment to personal development ensuring skills are kept up to date
Statistics and statistical analysis	Maintain accurate records, statistics and accounts; interpret and present statistical information about performance	Use appropriate systems to record statistics and accounts, e.g. databases, spreadsheets	Record statistical data relating to housekeeping activities
Subject knowledge	Demonstrate broad, in-depth, and up-to-date knowledge of pertinent fields relevant to the population served	Demonstrate a knowledge of the area of specialism	Look for opportunities to use and expand knowledge, skills, and experience
Training and development	Provide opportunities for professional growth and development of staff to enhance performance and skills	Update skills using appropriate methods and techniques	Take responsibility for self-development

Table 1.2	Examples of LIS competencies at professional, paraprofessional and non-professional level (Cont'd)

	Staff skill level		
Competence	Professional	Paraprofessional	Non-professional
User services – development and provision of information services and products	Assess the information needs of the population served and design a value-added service to meet those needs	Identify the community served and provide library services to meet user needs	Demonstrate a commitment to help others through customer care
Web and Internet	Exploit the use of the Web and Internet for networking, dissemination of information and as a source of information	Develop, create and maintain the library website using appropriate languages and scripts, e.g. HTML, JAVA, ensuring currency of data	Navigate the Internet and Web for sources of information using various functions and tools

- *Attributes*: That which can be predicated of anything; a quality or property; a virtue; an accessory.

- *Behaviours*: Good manners; general course of life; treatment of others; manner of action; activity of a person especially measurable for its effect.

- *Characteristic*: That which marks the aggregate of peculiar qualities that constitute personal or national individuality.

- *Competence*: Suitability, fitness, efficiency, capacity, capability, ability, knowledge, behaviours sufficiency, legal power; can be demonstrated.

- *Knowledge*: That which is known, information, instruction, enlightenment, learning, assured belief, acquaintance. What people know about specific topics.

- *Knowledge base*: Collection of specialist knowledge formulated for use especially in expert systems.

- *Motives*: Unconscious thoughts and preferences that drive behaviour, because behaviours are a source of satisfaction.

- *Self-image*: Individual's view of his/her own personality and ability, the views that people have of themselves.

- *Skill*: Expertness, craft or accomplishments, aptitude and competence appropriate for a particular job.

- *Social role*: Image that the individual displays in public. It represents what the person thinks is important and reflects the values of that person.

- *Traits*: Distinguishing features, enduring, habitual characteristics of people, reflecting the way in which we tend to describe people, e.g. flexible, reliable.

The competencies outlined in the table should be supplemented at the organisational level by local circumstances. It is recognised that many LIS professionals already possess some of the competencies listed. A clear route for progression needs to be built into any developmental programme. Where possible, professionals should be able to progress to an advanced level of skills.

Summary

Competencies are dynamic in that they must change and develop as the organisation's remit evolves. For an organisation or profession to survive, it must be able to deliver services that are required both now and in the future. All staff are expected to perform their work in a professional capacity, even if they are not professionally qualified. Their work should always meet the minimum standard defined for the task. Where librarians are concerned, although many traditional skills will be required, they must be able to adapt to ensure that the library services stay fit for purpose and their competencies fit for practice.

2

Training needs analysis

Introduction

For a learning organisation to grow and develop, its staff must have the necessary skills and knowledge to deliver the services required, both now and in the future. To ensure that workforce stays fit for purpose and fit for practice, an organisation must have an effective training and development strategy that addresses any performance gaps or deficiencies in the workplace.

A training needs analysis is the process of gathering information and interpreting data to identify the performance areas for improvement within an organisation, whether as a corporate entity or at an individual level.

Training needs may be divided into three levels:

- *Macro – organisational*: Corporate needs, e.g. culture, policy and procedures, performance indicators, target-setting.

- *Departmental – team*: Multi-skilled, e.g. service delivery, administrative, health and safety.

- *Micro – individual*: Job performance with satisfactory outcomes meeting minimum requirements.

Training needs are normally linked to competencies, which define the minimum standards required to deliver a satisfactory performance. In any work role, each task is broken down into sub-tasks and the key elements identified in accordance with a set of standards. The organisation, team or individual performance is then assessed against these prescribed standards or competencies. A training need is identified where performance delivery falls below or fails to meet the prescribe standard.

Training needs exist when there are gaps in skills and knowledge needed to perform certain tasks. These gaps occur as a result of many factors:

- Organisational
    - responding to demands of business;
    - changes in the workplace.
- Team
    - promotion;
    - new staff.
- Individual

    - deficiencies in performance, e.g. below standard;
    - refreshing or updating skills through continuous professional development.

Identifying level, mode and criticality

Whatever method is used to define training needs (e.g. see Figure 2.1), the outcome must indicate actual needs rather than a wish list. It is no good training someone on a financial package, for example, if those skills are not going to be used for, say, another year or more. Once the needs have been determined, the next step is to decide on the level and preferred mode of learning and the criticality of the training.

Figure 2.1 Training needs analysis approach

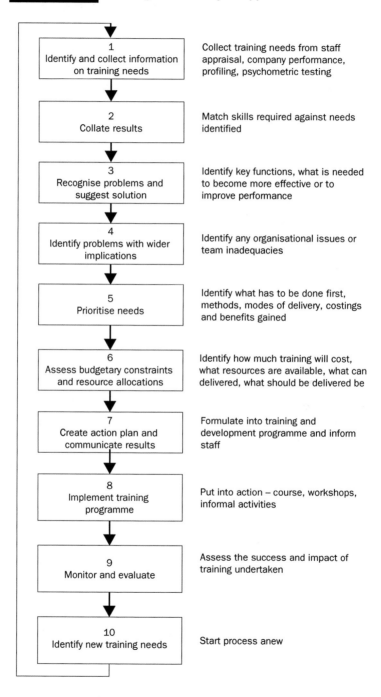

1 – Identify and collect information on training needs	Collect training needs from staff appraisal, company performance, profiling, psychometric testing
2 – Collate results	Match skills required against needs identified
3 – Recognise problems and suggest solution	Identify key functions, what is needed to become more effective or to improve performance
4 – Identify problems with wider implications	Identify any organisational issues or team inadequacies
5 – Prioritise needs	Identify what has to be done first, methods, modes of delivery, costings and benefits gained
6 – Assess budgetary constraints and resource allocations	Identify how much training will cost, what resources are available, what can delivered, what should be delivered be
7 – Create action plan and communicate results	Formulate into training and development programme and inform staff
8 – Implement training programme	Put into action – course, workshops, informal activities
9 – Monitor and evaluate	Assess the success and impact of training undertaken
10 – Identify new training needs	Start process anew

The level and complexity of the training relates to the amount of knowledge needed by the individual to perform the work task or competency satisfactorily. For example, a manager will require greater understanding of the recruitment process than a more junior officer, while someone working in a para-professional role will need more in-depth knowledge about searching skills than a non-professional. The levels are normally seen as progressive, that is, it is necessary to master efficiency at each level before moving on to the next stage.

- *Beginner*: Little knowledge, expertise or understanding.

- *Intermediate*: Some knowledge, expertise and understanding.

- *Advanced*: Lots of experience and expertise; looking at specialist areas.

The complexity of the task and the competence needed to perform the task will dictate the level to which the individual will need to be trained. For a new incumbent, it may be necessary to progress through all levels before becoming competent.

Training tends to be divided into two categories: formal and conventional, or informal non-conventional. The former focuses on traditional courses and workshops that are instructor-led in a classroom-based approach, where an individual interacts with other participants. The latter uses a range of tools and methods. These may be workbooks, e-learning, mentoring, on the job training or shadowing. The actual format will depend upon a number of factors, such as cost, preferred learning style and availability of training. Another factor influencing the mode of learning is the time taken to complete the training. This may vary from four 15-minute mentoring sessions, a half-day workshop, six-week shadowing to a two-year long distance learning course.

The criticality factor in training needs revolves around the urgency of the action to undertake and the completion of training. The CUED acronym is a useful mnemonic when assigning criticality factors (terminology may vary in different organisations.) Although there are no defined timescales, a rule of thumb suggests the following timescales for completing the training:

- *Critical*: within the next 1–12 weeks.

- *Urgent*: within the next 3–5 months.

- *Essential*: within the next 6–9 months.

- *Desirable*: within the next 12 months.

'Critical' indicates that the training is crucial to the work role or service delivery. Where a person's training has been classified as critical, the impact of not achieving within the time scale must be assessed, as it is likely to have cost implications or severely impair performance or output. An example would be training staff how to use new software for issuing material.

In the other categories, if the training is not completed within the designated period, it usually moves up one level until it becomes critical.

The 'desirable' category tends to describe needs that, over a period of time, will either change criticality or become irrelevant and therefore unnecessary. Desirable needs must be seen to have a value-added impact at the end of the training.

Appendix A presents an example training needs analysis document from the London Library and Information Development Unit. This details the codes indicating the type, methods, urgency and level of training required.

Summary

To enable an organisation to produce a meaningful training and development programme, it must have constructive feedback from the staff as to their present requirements and projected future needs. This may be gleaned from a number of sources, such as staff appraisal, observation or the introduction of new equipment to changes in practices. It is important to establish what training is required, the preferred format (formal versus informal), the level (beginner, intermediate, advanced), the urgency (critical, urgent, essential, desirable) and how soon it needs to be completed. It is essential that all training activities are evaluated as to their relevance in the workplace, their effectiveness in closing the skills gaps and ensuring the workforce is fully competent.

3

Performance appraisal

Introduction

Performance appraisals are referred to by an array of names, such as staff appraisals, individual performance assessment, progress planning, job reviews and annual reviews. Some appraisal systems are linked to annual pay awards, with the coming year's salary dependent on the outcome of the review. Others may include personality or psychometric testing.

Appraisals tend to be a rather emotive subject, partly because they are often poorly done. People view them with dread, feeling they have been thrust on them, frequently as part of government policy (in many countries, workers are legally required to have appraisals). The overarching reason for conducting appraisals is to develop staff to ensure they stay fit for purpose and fit for the future. Appraisals can be used to provide constructive feedback, undertake remedial action, maintain standards, improve performance, identify training gaps, increase motivation, as well as to set objectives for the coming year.

There are questions as to who should conduct the appraisal, for example, the immediate line manager, senior line manager (sometimes referred to as grandparent), project manager or head of department. Whoever conducts the review must be familiar with the appraisee's work. The success of the annual review depends on the skills of those carrying out the appraisal. The assessment of performance must be fair, non-judgmental and unbiased. This means giving time and commitment to conduct the process properly. Good preparation, listening and following through are crucial to the outcome. Both appraiser and appraisee need to be trained in the art of the appraisal technique.

Appraisal is a two-way conversation allowing for upward and downward feedback. It is a discussion not an interview. The appraisal is not to be used to cast blame, to criticise the person, or to be influenced by something that went wrong last week. If the performance has been consistently bad throughout the year, the line manager or appraiser should have dealt with it before the appraisal. Consistently poor performance may be a cause for disciplinary action or even dismissal.

Types of appraisal

There are various ways in which appraisal can be conducted, from a single review by a senior manager to multi-level, multi-source appraisal, such as full-circle or 360-degree appraisal. Appraisal will include an element of self-assessment for the individual. All forms of appraisal have benefits and drawbacks.

Appraisal by line manager

Appraisal is conducted between the appraisee and the line manager (immediate or senior line manager). The line manager may seek views from other staff but not as a formalised procedure. Table 3.1 presents the advantages and disadvantages of line manager appraisal.

| Table 3.1 | Advantages and disadvantages of appraisal by line manager |

Advantages	Disadvantages
Line manager knows employee's work	May be geographically separated so less familiar with day-to-day work
Good managers will be impartial and fair	May be unfamiliar with work activities or specialism
Senior line manager may be more objective as removed from day-to-day operations	May be in different discipline so less able to comment on specific skills or competencies
Regular contact with member of staff	

In 90-degree reviews, the views of peers are sought as part of the procedure. Peers are colleagues working at the same level and utilising similar skills. This type of appraisal may be used where project work is concerned or staff are working in multi-professional teams.

360-degree appraisal

The 360-degree appraisal usually involves superiors, such as line manager and senior staff, peers (colleagues working at same or similar level), subordinates and customers. The 360-degree appraisal has been likened to a jury. Colleagues are asked to comment on a series of statements, normally using a rating scale to assess aspects of the individual's performance, for example, with respect to team-working or time-keeping. Customers will be carefully selected to provide feedback. For instance, in a healthcare setting, regular users of the library service may be doctors or nurses, or library committee members. The results are then analysed and fed back to the individual during the appraisal. The appraisee also undertakes a self-assessment of the previous year's performance.

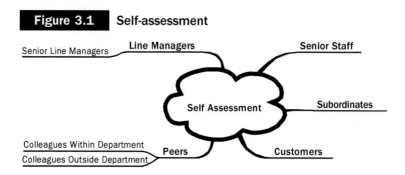

Figure 3.1   Self-assessment

Organisational policy will dictate whether third-party ratings and comments, given as feedback during the appraisal discussion, should be anonymised or not. Anonymity will encourage a more open and honest review, however, confidentiality may leave the appraisee trying to identify who said what (particularly where negative comments have been made). The whole process could involve up to ten people commenting on an individual's performance. This has to be repeated for each member of staff. Figure 3.1 illustrates the self-assessment aspect of this type of appraisal. Table 3.2 presents the advantages and disadvantages of 360-degree appraisal.

Ratings

Ratings use a common yardstick that applies across an organisation to indicate the standards expected of a post holder. The 'rules' of rating systems state that there should never be more than seven points on which to rate the appraisee. Using an even-numbered scale prevents middle-of-the-road marking. Anchor points should always be used, for example, excellent – very good – good – satisfactory – poor – unsatisfactory. Some appraisal systems indicate the previous year's ratings, either to show consistency, improvement or decline in performance. Some rating scales may not be

Table 3.2 Advantages and disadvantages of 360-degree appraisal

Advantages	Disadvantages
Seen as giving more rounded view of performance	Resentment at being judged by peers or subordinates
Empowers employees to exert some influence and give voice	Can be threatening and intimidating
Overcomes bias of one person	Does not imply more objective assessment or more meaningful outcome
May be effective where common skills mix is the same as the appraiser's	Time-consuming and costly – involves many people for each person
Some skills and competencies are best judged by peers	May be hidden agenda
Wider involvement helps to engender the learning culture of the organisation	Appraisal fatigue
Feedback from peers tends to enhance self-development	Peer rating usually subjective, conflict may colour judgment
Increases accountability of staff to their customers	May be gender, ethnic or cultural bias
	May not be effective in a multidisciplinary team where the skills vary

applicable to certain grades, for example, uniform, manual handling. Figure 3.2 provides three examples of how ratings systems might be applied. Table 3.3 presents the advantages and disadvantages of using ratings for appraisal.

Competencies related appraisal

Competence is the *minimum* level of performance expected of a member of staff to carry out the designated work role or task effectively and efficiently. Competencies underlie the behaviours thought necessary to achieve a desired outcome.

Figure 3.2 Examples of ratings systems

Topic	Always	Often	Occasionally	Never
e.g. Time keeping				

Topic	Excellent	Very Good	Good	Satisfactory	Poor	Unsatisfactory
e.g. Time keeping						

Topic	1	2	3	4	5	6
e.g. Time keeping						

1	Exceeds standards is all respects
2	Exceeds standards in most respects
3	Exceeds standards in some respects
4	Meet standards
5	Fails to meet most standards
6	Fails to meet standards

Table 3.3 Advantages and disadvantages of using ratings

Advantages	Disadvantages
Easily understood	Some managers never use the top rating on principle that no-one is 'perfect' or that a top performance cannot be maintained
Can be analysed	Subjectivity leads to distortion and bias
Can be used for comparison	One positive attribute can colour all the other areas
	Favouritism possible
	Not applied equally by appraisers

A competency is something that can be demonstrated, where it is clear when the behaviour outcome is successful, i.e. something a person can or cannot do. Table 3.4 presents the advantages and disadvantages of this type of appraisal.

| Table 3.4 | Advantages and disadvantages of competencies related appraisals |

Advantages	Disadvantages
More behaviourally based	Advantages are lost if linked to rewards
Less likely to generate conflict	Limited opportunity to compare performance
More concerned with long term	

Performance related pay

In the 1990s, many organisations severed the link between appraisal and performance related pay (PRP). Increases to staff salaries were awarded on merit and determined by results of the appraisal. This can represent anything from a 3 to 20 per cent increase, although the lower end of the scale is the norm. In other cases, staff may be given an incremental rise up one or two points on the salary scale. If company has a bad year, it may not be able to implement the pay awards. Table 3.5 presents the advantages and disadvantages of this type of appraisal.

| Table 3.5 | Advantages and disadvantages of performance related pay |

Advantages	Disadvantages
Strive to achieve or improve output	People often believe they have performed better than they have and deserve more money
Can be an incentive to work harder	Difference between perception and actual performance
	Some people work hard but little output or achievement
	Can be very costly to organisation
	Most people get less than expected or no increase at all

Appraisal process

In any performance appraisal, there are three components: preparation, discussion and follow-up.

Timing of appraisal tends either to be on the anniversary of joining the organisation or taking up the current appointment, or at a given time each year (often in the month before end of financial year). The former means appraisals will be staggered throughout the year, the latter is a top-heavy period for the appraisers. Any appraisal worth doing will take between two and three hours to complete.

Both the appraiser and the appraisee need to consider a number of issues in advance of the review. Each person should have the opportunity to see, if not complete, the (organisation's) appraisal form before the discussion. An example of an appraisal form is given in Appendix B. The outcomes of successful appraisal, and the barriers to successful appraisal are presented in Table 3.6.

Preparation

Give the appraisee a minimum of three weeks' notice to prepare for the appraisal. A lack of preparation on either side means the appraisal will be superficial.

Ideally, the appraisal room should be on neutral territory, for example, not the manager's office. The room needs to provide a quiet relaxed atmosphere, where the appraisal can be carried out without any interruptions (e.g. telephone). Although the appraisal is a formal activity, the discussion itself should be a free-flowing conversation.

Both parties need to have copies of the last appraisal, job description, person specification and any other documents deemed necessary.

Table 3.6	Barriers and successful appraisals
Barriers to effective appraisal	**Successful appraisal**
Lack of time and commitment	Improved performance
Poor planning	Increased motivation
Too subjective	Identifying training need
Seeing process as a waste of time	Recognising potential
Lack of training	Focus on career development
Fear/seen as punishment	Constructive feedback
One-way conversation	Praise/reward
Being over-generous with praise – may not be justified	Future expectations
Misusing the appraisal to make subordinate look better	Problem solving
Not wanting to mark staff down	Improved working relationships
Rewarding staff who have made no significant improvement but have worked hard	Formal record of progress and achievements of staff

Reflection

Appraisals are used to assess an individual's performance against the previous year's objectives, as well as setting new objectives for the coming 12 months.

Both the appraiser and appraisee need to reflect on:

- Previous year's objectives – have they been met?
- Work profile/job description – are there any significant changes?
- Competence levels – appropriate to the post, organisational requirement.
- Training and development completed in the last 12 months;

- topics;
- usefulness.
- Review of previous 12 months;

  - assess the achievements of the last 12 months, and find something to praise;
  - assess any difficulties encountered in the last 12 months, and the reasons for these difficulties. Use constructively, e.g. as learning experience, problem solving.

Discussion

If an appraisal is to be successful, then the elements of trust and confidentiality, honesty and open dialogue must prevail. It is important that the appraisee learns how to receive constructive feedback whether as praise or criticism. The most constructive feedback comes from those with whom the appraisee works on a daily basis.

An effective appraisal means that the appraisee will be doing least two-thirds of the talking. An important part of the process for the appraiser is to manage the silence, so as to give the appraisee time to think. An effective use of the time can be considered as:

> 66% appraisee talking → 33% appraisee listening → 1% managing the silence
> 66% appraiser listening → 33% appraiser talking → 1% managing the silence

The appraiser should start by restating the purpose, setting the scene and agreeing the agenda. The review is in four parts:

- reflection and constructive feedback;
- looking forward;

- agreeing the action plan;
- following-up.

Each section of the appraisal must be completed before moving on to the next area. The appraiser needs to summarise the discussion and ensure there are no loose ends. Anything more to be said? Have all the points been covered?

Reflection and feedback

The review begins by reflecting back on the previous year's objectives (were they met?) and training undertaken (how beneficial?). Always start with something positive, such as asking the appraisee to focus on achievements and successes. The appraiser needs to find something, no matter how small, to praise. This could be answering a complex enquiry, completion of a project, consistency in output or mastering a new skill.

Encourage the appraisee to reflect on:

- real circumstances and actual behaviour;
- perception of self;
- perception by others;
- effect that the appraisee has on others;
- blind spots (perceived or actual).

Feedback on performance can be described with the mnemonics of LIFE and DEATH. Thus, for positive feedback:

- *Learning* from experience.
- *Improvement* in performance.
- *Favourable* comments about work.
- *Effectiveness* in service.

For negative feedback and criticism:

- *Details* of poor performance.

- *Effects* on the service, customers or colleagues.

- *Action* to be taken.

- *Timescale* for improvements (one month, three-month review).

- *How* will you act if there is insufficient improvement?

In looking at the negative aspects and difficulties encountered, the appraisal should seek to establish how these affected performance and why they occurred. The difficulties may be internal, such as computer downtime, or external, such as non-delivery of supplies. Often the appraisee can be the harshest critic. Constructive negative feedback is about redressing the inadequacies of poor performance. It is not a character assassination.

Negative criticisms must be handled sensitively:

- Use statements that present criticism in a supportive way
  - identify behaviours that are in need of change;
  - concentrate on what can be changed.
- Use feeling words (angry, excited, resent, afraid)
  - acknowledge personal or emotional issues;
  - deal with emotions and grudges.
- Do not use judgmental words
  - good, bad, right, wrong, immature, should not.
- Describe specific instances of observed behaviour
  - identify problem areas;
  - give concrete examples to support points.
- Be constructive

  – offer suggestions about learning from mistakes or how to overcome difficulties;

  – provide a realistic perception of competencies.

An appraisal must not be used as a substitute for disciplinary matters. Where an individual's performance has been shown to be inadequate over a prolonged period, the situation must be confronted and managed. Where deficiencies have been noted, poor performers must be given the opportunity to improve. All options should be considered. The first step is to identify the *what* and *why*. Are there generic issues that relate to the organisation? Or external factors to be considered?

  Causes of poor performance include:

- lack of training;
- lack of understanding;
- lack of motivation;
- pressure;
- boredom;
- working above or below capability;
- illness;
- missing targets;
- expectations not met;
- fast pace of change;
- personal agenda;
- unrealistic objectives;
- personality or job clashes;
- bullying.

The appraiser needs to present the appraisee with conclusive evidence of consistent and unacceptable behaviour, such as carelessness, time-keeping, attitude towards customers, breeches in safety or security, in line with the DEATH mnemonic, described previously.

In some cases, providing the appraisee with better training or perhaps explaining the procedure in more detail can rectify the situation. If, after several warnings and opportunities, there is no improvement in performance, then the matter may be referred for disciplinary action or dismissal.

Looking forward

In looking forward, the appraisee should be asked to suggest how performance could be improved, what standards are expected and whether there are any gaps in learning to be addressed. It is important to ascertain what help or support the appraisee needs from the appraiser.

Appraisals are not done in isolation; they are integrally linked to progress within the team, department and the organisation. The appraiser needs to be mindful of developments within the organisation – where it is going, changes, the skills mix, products and services – and ensure that the appraisee's objectives match organisational requirements.

Agreeing the action plan

The penultimate part of the appraisal is to create an action plan by identifying the objectives and developmental activities required for the coming year. It is too easy to send staff on 'another training course', so explore different training methods to stimulate and inspire the person. Setting challenging goals and giving the individual ownership of their development are generally seen to increase motivation.

Use the SMART acronym when setting objectives:

- Specific/Stretching
- Measurable

- Achievable/Agreed
- Realistic
- Timebound

What is to be achieved in the next 12 months?

- Outline 3–5 SMART objectives
  - How will the objectives be achieved?
  - What methods will be used?
  - How will success be measured?
  - How will the difficulties be overcome?
- Draw up a personal development plan for the next 12 months.
- Define the training and development requirements:
  - Topic e.g. thesaurus construction
  - Level e.g. intermediate
  - Method e.g. one-to-one
  - Urgency e.g. within 6 months
  - Expected outcomes
  - List the competencies and skills required to complete the work (in line with organisational needs)
- Agree performance related pay if part of appraisal.

Advantages and disadvantages of appraisal by objectives are presented in Table 3.7.

Summarising discussion

In bringing the appraisal to its conclusion, the appraiser needs to summarise the agreed action points, such as objectives, training, follow-up issues. They must check back with the appraisee that there are no outstanding issues or

Table 3.7	Advantages and disadvantages of appraisal by objectives

Advantages	Disadvantages
Objectivity	Difficult to make comparisons
Motivational	Objective may not be 'challenging'
Participative	External factors may change role so objective become irrelevant

points for clarification. Before leaving the room, interim review dates should be set, for example, next three, six and nine months. It is imperative that the appraisal ends on a good note, with the appraisee feeling inspired, positive or encouraged.

Follow-up

The following actions need to be completed as soon as possible after the appraisal.

Documentation

Only keep what is required for the purpose of appraisal, such as the form and personal development plan. The appraisal form should be a quality record that is written up at the time or immediately after the appraisal. It needs be signed and dated by all the relevant parties, for example, appraiser, appraisee, senior line manager, with comments made as appropriate. In accordance with organisational procedure, the form and copies thereof, should be held on the relevant files (e.g. by personnel, by appraisee, by appraiser). All documentation must comply with domestic legislation for confidentiality and privacy, for example, data protection.

Monitoring progress

Although the appraisal has a formal annual element, provisions need to be enacted to ensure that:

- the appraisee is on target to meet the objectives;
- training and development arrangements have been set in motion;
- skills and competencies match organisational requirements;
- interim review meetings are held to discuss progress.

Common mistakes in appraisals include:

- halo effect;
- working hard but not productive;
- extremes of rating – too harsh, too soft, bias;
- talking too much;
- inadequate briefing and reparation;
- prejudging;
- insufficient time for discussion;
- wrong time and place;
- interruptions;
- too subjective/not factual or evidential;
- offering opinions;
- overstating weaknesses or strengths;
- ignoring special circumstances;
- dismissive of concept of appraisal;
- misunderstanding of system/situation/ conversation;
- becoming too personal;
- poor communications;

- personality or job clash;
- failing to complete the process;
- not following up on action points;
- not completing paperwork.

Summary

Successful outcomes may be measured at the appraisee, appraiser and organisational level:

- *Appraisee*: People feel more responsibility for something they have helped to create. Commitment to completing a given task, reaching a desired outcome or effectively utilising skills, experience and expertise can be just as rewarding as offering a financial incentive.

- *Appraiser*: Steering the appraisee in the right direction brings enormous benefits, such as improved performance and productivity. Acknowledging the productive working of the appraisee encourages self-development and learning.

- *Organisational*: A satisfied workforce is likely to become more flexible and adaptable to change. By improving relationships and providing a better quality of life in the workplace, a caring organisation will be able to make better use of its staff, time and resources.

Although appraisal has become more sophisticated, in many instances it is still poorly conducted. A formal appraisal once a year is no substitute for daily contact with staff. Where appraisals are carried out effectively, they will recognise the achievements and successes of the individual. Rewards do not have to be financial. Staff can be motivated by many other factors, from increased responsibility and greater autonomy to enhanced career options and more flexible working arrangements.

Both appraiser and appraisee must be trained in appraisal technique. Appraiser training includes:

- appraisal review and documentation;
- setting the scene – what is appraisal and the reason for it;
- paperwork to be completed;
- structure and timing;
- allaying anxiety;
- setting SMART objectives;
- dealing with diversity – cultural, ethnic, gender, disability, discrimination;
- problem solving;
- giving and receiving feedback;
- obtaining information;
- motivating;
- coaching/mentoring;
- listening, observation and questioning techniques.

Appraisee training includes:

- background briefing;
- how to prepare;
- guidance on objective;
- discussion on self-assessment;
- giving and receiving feedback;
- combating anxieties;
- assertiveness training;
- responding to criticism;

- how to get action;
- moving forward.

Personal development plans

What is a personal development plan?

Personal development plans (PDPs) may be known by different names, such as learning contracts, personal audits, personal action plans, learner profiling, or learning agreements.

According to the UK Quality Assurance Agency, a PDP is a 'structured and supported process undertaken by an individual to reflect upon their own learning, performance and/or achievement and to plan for their personal, educational and career development' (Quality Assurance Agency, 2004).

A PDP creates a clear plan of action for an individual to complete over a given period. The plan will cover areas of learning, objectives or goal setting, as well as defining gaps in development. Responsibility and ownership for the learning rest with the individual.

PDPs require individuals to look at their 'whole life picture'. Although the employer will only be interested in those parts of the plan that relate specifically to the work scenario, the employee should be thinking more widely about personal vision, goals and development. This holistic view embraces both professional and personal aspirations. Work activities will include career and learning, while home and leisure covers family matters, physical health, spiritual elements and finances.

PDPs are about extending, stretching, testing and growing the individual. It is important to remember that personal development is an ongoing process with no finite end. It recognises that personal potential has no limits and that everything successful has the potential to be improved. There is no set formula for creating a personal development plan; Figure 3.3 presents a model for a PDP, and an example of a template is given in Figure 3.4.

A PDP must be written with honesty, integrity and constructive thought. Many people find it difficult to talk about themselves. They often focus on their negative elements rather than positive attributes. In career terms, you are answerable to yourself for your achievements.

What are the benefits of a PDP?

Listed below are some of the benefits for the organisation that come from supporting staff personal development:

- becoming a learning organisation – learning is integral to organisational development and growth;
- increasing staff motivation;
- actioning inconsistencies and providing a forum for continuous improvement of staff;
- ensuring that the employees' skills are up to date and relevant to the organisation;
- increasing effectiveness and efficiency;
- sharing organisational goals, culture and understanding.

Individual benefits include:

- increasing confidence and feeling valued;
- addressing the gaps in learning and improving competence;
- giving focus and direction for a period of time;
- recording achievements and progress, and measuring against objectives;

Figure 3.3 Personal development plan cycle

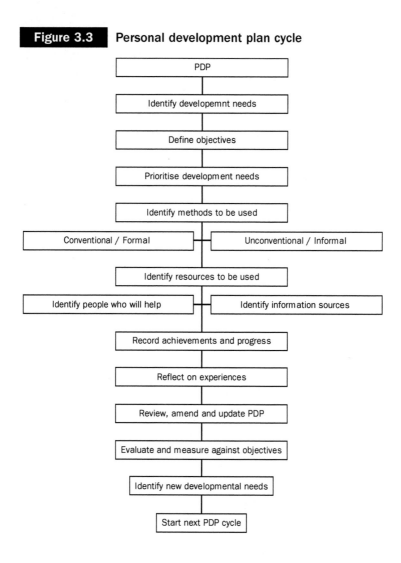

- encouraging reflective practice – successes and difficulties;

- energising individuals to try new ventures and challenges;

- maximising on opportunities.

Figure 3.4 Personal development plan – example

Your name						
Mentor's name						
Date agreed		Date reviewed		Date reviewed		
Developmental need	Proposed action	Anticipated outcome	Benefit gained	People who will help	Information sources	Timescale
Other actions						
Other actions						
Mentor's signature						

Performance

Within the workplace, PDPs are often linked to staff performance or staff appraisals. They frequently form the basis on which the forthcoming year's objectives are set. For the employer, PDPs are intrinsically linked to organisational objectives such as maximising individual performance, strengthening the team and capitalising on intellectual capability (see also performance appraisal). The individual is likely to share the contents of the PDP with colleagues, as they may be key figures in helping the employee achieve the objectives.

The individual's vision should be about achieving maximum potential, and preparing to do what is necessary to achieve personal goals. Questions to be asked include: Where do I want to go? How will I get there? What support do I need? Who will help me achieve my ambition? Who will hinder my development? What obstacles are in my way? Is this part of something bigger? Do my aspirations conflict with other interests or work? Do I have the motivation, endurance and willpower to succeed?

Objective setting

Development plans require a number of objectives to be set (objectives are sometimes referred to as goals, targets or aims). The objectives should be clear statements of what can be achieved in the designated period, for example, 12 months, and limited in number (e.g. 3–5 objectives). The plan is not a wish list. The objectives should be SMART.

It is preferable to write the objectives using action words like 'create', 'analyse', 'evaluate', 'demonstrate'; for example, 'analyse the information audit questionnaire and present the results to the executive board'. Active objectives are easier to measure. This does not preclude using the passive voice, for example, 'list the reading books for 6–8-year olds', but makes measuring the objectives more difficult. How do you measure the list? By the length? Is it selective? Did you do anything with the list once it was compiled?

In preparing a plan of action, it is always easiest to start with what you know and can handle relatively simply. Break all the tasks or challenges that you have set yourself into bite-size chunks. Start by making small changes, such as becoming more efficient, working smarter or eliminating procrastination. Treat new situations as a challenge not a threat, and consider the consequences of any changes that you make.

Timescales

The norm is to set PDP objectives for a 12-month period, but an interim and long-term plan should be considered. PDPs need to be thought of in three stages: short term, for example, what has to happen in the next 3–6 months; medium term, for example, what are my aspirations for the next 12 months; and long term, say 1–3 years, for example, is my plan part of something bigger, such as studying for a degree or travelling the world?

Recording achievements and evaluating objectives

It is important to keep a record of all developmental activities. The log should indicate what training was undertaken. This will include formal training, such as courses and other non-conventional formats, such as coaching sessions. A key element of the plan is the individual's ability to turn theory into practice and to reflect upon the outcome. So the issues to be addressed are, 'What was the value of the learning experience?', 'How was it applied?' and 'What benefits were gained?'

The PDP needs to be periodically reviewed, amended and updated. Objectives must be measurable, for example, did I analyse the information audit and to whom did I present the findings?

It may be helpful to ask a series of questions:

- What tasks have been achieved or completed?

- What learning has come from these activities?

- Are there clear links between theory and practice

- What benefits have been gained during the period in question?

- What new needs have been identified?

Conclusion

Personal development plans form a cycle of continuous professional and personal development. They are part of a long-term career development strategy. PDPs recognise the need for individuals to take control of their own learning. They emphasise the importance of reflective practice and being able to relate theory to practice. If PDPs are to be successful, individuals must be able to see tangible benefits, whether these may be acquiring new skills, achieving a personal goal, gaining confidence or improving performance.

4

Curriculum vitae and interviewing tips

Introduction

A curriculum vitae (CV) is important as it is usually the first thing that a potential employer sees and it should be an integral part of a continuous professional development (CPD) portfolio. The CV is your opportunity to market yourself, to outline your accomplishments and achievements. The construction of the CV says something about you, so it must be eye-catching and worthy of following up. Modesty, humbleness or timidity will not impress the potential employer.

Practices and conventions relating to content, level of detail and format of the CV vary between countries. What is applicable in the USA may differ from the requirements in Australia or the UK.

Impressing the employer

The importance of making an immediate impact is paramount in the recruitment process, which is, usually, select, consider further or reject. Your CV has ten seconds in which to grab the employer's attention. Often, a cursory glance will consign the poorly presented CV to the bin without a second look.

What is it that the employer wants to know about you?

- Ability and capability
  - potential to carry out a range of tasks and activities;
  - managerial awareness.
- Attitude
  - flexibility;
  - willingness.
- Employability
  - suitability for the job;
  - right fit (fit for purpose, fit for the future, fit as team player).
- Knowledge
  - experience and qualifications;
  - personal attributes that will contribute to the organisation;
  - communication and interpersonal skills
  - managerial and financial.
- Skills
  - expertise and competencies;
  - skills appropriate to tasks (at least 85 per cent of new job) (see also LIS competencies);
  - areas of specialisation, e.g. cataloguing, web design, IT.

Preparation

The CV must be up-to-date and reflective of your experience and expertise. Time should be taken to prepare the CV and, where necessary, tailor according to the job specification. It may be prudent to have two or three CVs, perhaps emphasising different aspects of your skills and expertise. For instance, one CV may reflect your searching skills while another might concentrate on your ability as a trainer.

Unless specifically requested, there is no set practice as to whether references should be given at the time of application. The normal procedure is to give two referees, one of which should be your current or most recent employer. (If you are a recent school or college leaver then use a tutor or teacher.) You must use people who are able to comment on your technical and managerial skills, personal attributes and your performance. Ensure that the people have agreed to give you a reference and notify each referee when you apply for a new position (unless told otherwise).

Content

- Preferably no more than two pages, maximum four pages.
- Is the CV clear about
  - who you are?
  - what you have to offer?
  - why the employer should employ you?
- Are there any gaps in the employment history – why?
- Is your name on every page (header or footer)?

Page 1: key information

Key information should include:

- personal information at top of page;
- name;

- address;

- contact point – telephone (home/work); fax; e-mail;

- academic/professional post nominals qualifications, e.g. MA PhD MCLIP;

- personal attributes;

- professional skills and competencies (main selling point);

- current (or last) employment, i.e. job title and dates and a brief scenario – adequate information but not life history.

Page 2: supporting information

All historical information should be on the second page and given in reverse chronological order, i.e. most recent first to oldest. This information should include:

- employment history (last ten years only);
  - check dates of all prior employment;
  - ensure there are no gaps;

- relevant training/appropriate courses/current study, e.g. MA;

- recent achievements (if relevant to employer);

- professional membership/involvement;

- publications – if you have written any articles, you may wish to list these on a separate page;

- education
  - schools/colleges and dates;
  - qualifications – brief resumé;

- other factors, if relevant, including
  - disabilities which may need to be taken into account;
  - extracurricular involvement that shows endeavour, e.g. first aid;
  - anything else that is going to impress the prospective employer.
- Factors to omit (unless specifically requested to include):
  - date of birth and age, marital status, family details;
  - gender and ethnic and other similar personal information;
  - height and weight;
  - salary history.

Beware of areas that might cause controversy, such as political alliances, some trade union activities, dangerous sports or strong opinions.

Page 3: references

It is recommended that you give the referees' details on a separate sheet, and include:

- name;
- position held;
- company/organisation;
- address;
- telephone, fax;
- e-mail, website;
- relationship, e.g. line manager, tutor.

Presentation and format of the CV

When you are composing your CV, use action verbs and write short phrases that describe what you have done. Enlarge upon your experience, expertise and skills. Do not write your life story or compose large chunks of text – be concise and specific. Arrange the skills and action points in order of relevance to the position for which you are applying.

Good and bad practices

Do:

- Show clear thinking, and a well thought out, easy to read, logical order.
- Write up to two pages for the CV (using the third and fourth pages for publications/references).
- Tailor your CV for each post.
- Use white space around border.
- Use a 12-point font.
- Use a clear typeface, e.g. Arial, Helvetica or Times New Roman.
- Limit use of embellishments and font size – use to emphasise headings only.
- Give sharp and precise details.
- Use action words, e.g. 'managed project', rather than passive terms, e.g. 'thought about project briefing' (Table 4.1 presents a list of useful action words, Table 4.2 gives examples of passive words).
- Use indentation and bullet points.
- Cite chronologically with the most recent first.

Table 4.1   Action words for CVs

Achieved	Converted	Formed	Modernised
Acquired	Corrected	Formulated	Monitored
Activated	Counselled	Generated	Negotiated
Addressed	Created	Guided	Obtained
Administered	Cultivated	Hired	Operated
Advised	Decentralised	Implemented	Organised
Analysed	Decreased	Improved	Originated
Anticipated	Defined	Improvised	Performed
Appointed	Demonstrated	Increased	Pioneered
Appraised	Designed	Initiated	Planned
Approved	Determined	Inspired	Prepared
Arranged	Developed	Inspected	Presented
Assessed	Devised	Instigated	Prevented
Audited	Directed	Instructed	Proceeded
Augmented	Documented	Innovated	Procured
Averted	Doubled	Insured	Produced
Avoided	Edited	Interpreted	Programmed
Bought	Effected	Interviewed	Promoted
Built	Eliminated	Introduced	Proved
Computed	Employed	Invented	Provided
Catalysed	Enforced	Investigated	Published
Centralised	Engineered	Launched	Purchased
Collaborated	Established	Led	Recommended
Combined	Estimated	Lightened	Recruited
Composed	Evaluated	Liquidated	Redesigned
Conceived	Executed	Localised	Reduced
Concluded	Expanded	Located	Regulated
Condensed	Expedited	Maintained	Rejected
Conducted	Extracted	Managed	Related
Consummated	Finalised	Marketed	Renegotiated
Controlled	Forecasted	Minimised	Reorganised

Table 4.1   Action words for CVs (*Cont'd*)

Reported	Settled	Streamlined	Tightened
Researched	Shaped	Studied	Traded
Resolved	Simplified	Supervised	Trained
Reviewed	Sold	Supported	Translated
Revised	Solved	Surpassed	Tripled
Revitalised	Specified	Surveyed	Vitalised
Saved	Staffed	Taught	Wrote
Scheduled	Standardised	Terminated	
Selected	Stimulated	Tested	

Table 4.2   Examples of passive words

Considered	Discussed	Listed	Visited
Described	Engaged	Thought	

- List employment – employer, dates, job title, brief resumé of responsibilities.
- Explain gaps in career history.
- Provide evidence of achievements.
- Show relevant qualifications such as degrees and professional qualifications.
- List relevant (recent) training.
- Use words that you are familiar with (use a dictionary).
- Maintain a consistent writing style – particularly with present and past tenses.
- If you begin a sentence with a number – write out all numbers between one and nine (e.g. two, three), but use numerals for all numbers 10 and above (e.g. 10, 15).

- Ensure your name and date appear on each page of the CV, e.g. in the header or footer.

- References – check all details are current – especially addresses, contact numbers and e-mail addresses.

- Print final copies of your CV on quality paper. Use the same colour and type of paper (white or cream) for CV, cover letter and envelope.

- Print on one side of the paper only.

- Double-check everything, particularly the grammar and spelling.

- Save as a Word document, especially if you are circulating your CV via e-mail, you must ensure that recipient is able to open your file, and read the document.

Do not:

- Submit more than three pages.

- Overcrowd, muddle, confuse, complicate.

- Use cluttered or fancy layout.

- Use fonts smaller than 11-point or larger than 14-point.

- Overuse fonts or fonts that are difficult to read, e.g. Gothic.

- Overuse colours, capitalisation, italics, underlining, clip art or other embellishments.

- Mislead, exaggerate or tell lies.

- Write in a story style or use large blocks of text.

- Cite chronological details with oldest first.

- Omit evidence of output of achievements.

- Include irrelevant qualifications.

- List irrelevant or non-recent training.

- Include irrelevant details, e.g. family, hobbies.
- Use 'I' or 'my', e.g. 'I did this'.
- Pad out or exaggerate employment.
- Leave gaps unaccounted for, e.g. career breaks.
- Use abbreviations or acronyms unless you define them.
- Use jargon unless specific to your industry.
- Use the vernacular.
- Waste money on fancy folders or binders.
- Use coloured paper or other fancy stationery.
- Send in photocopies of the CV.
- Send in an old unamended CV.
- Submit an electronic format that might not be easy to open, e.g. ZIP file.
- Leave grammatical errors and spelling mistakes.

Checking your CV

It is inexcusable to have typing, spelling or grammatical errors in your CV, so have someone else proofread it for you.

Be aware of:

- Spelling mistakes
  - use the word processor's spell check function, but remember that it does not differentiate between correctly spelt words that are in the wrong context, e.g. 'form' instead of 'from'; 'affect' instead of 'effect'.
- Punctuation mistakes
  - correct use of punctuation;

- be consistent in your use of punctuation;
- avoid using exclamation marks to emphasise points.
- Grammatical mistakes
  - use present tense for current activities and past tense to explain previous work or employment;
  - capitalise all proper nouns.

Covering letter

A covering letter, attached to your CV, is highly recommended, even if you were not asked for one. If submitting an application form for a job, complete it and submit with a covering letter and a copy of your CV. *Never* put 'See attached CV'.

The letter needs to be short but focused, emphasising your suitability for the post. Clearly state the position that you are applying for, ensuring that you have the correct job title, and indicate where and when you saw it advertised. You will need to justify why you should be invited for an interview. Your letter should elaborate upon key skills or attributes that you will bring to the job, but do not repeat all the details from your CV. If references are not given on your CV, make sure that the prospective employer knows that this information is available on request.

An example of a covering letter is given in Appendix C. The format of the covering letter should be in accordance with the protocol of the candidate's own country or culture. Local etiquette needs to be observed for the opening salutation and the conventions for closing a letter. For instance, in the UK a letter starting 'Dear Sir' closes with 'Yours faithfully', while a letter starting 'Dear Mr Jones' finishes with 'Yours sincerely'.

The CV needs to have a good balance of white space and text (see Figure 4.1). Try holding your CV at a 45° angle – how do the white spaces and blocks of text complement each other? The effect should be pleasing to the eye (see Figure 4.2).

Figure 4.1   Use of white space on the CV

Figure 4.2 The 'wall test'

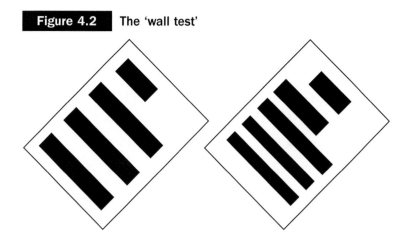

Interview tips

With acknowledgement to Octavia Jennings, Independent Careers Consultant, for the reproduction of the material taken from her interview handout.

Introduction

This section prepares you for the job interview. For some people, the experience of an interview either for a promotion or for a new post may be nothing more than a distant memory. Others may have attended an interview recently or sat on recruitment or promotion panels, conducted appraisals or interviewed candidates – if this is the case for you, the interview process will not be totally unfamiliar.

The specific areas explored in this section are:

- preparing yourself;
- types of interview;

- likely questions;
- difficult questions;
- structure of the interview;
- managing the interview.

Preparing yourself

Preparing for an interview either for a promotion or new post within your organisation (or a prospective employer) follows the same principles.

To help you prepare, consider the possible situations you may come across at interview and how you will approach the issue. It is important to be well prepared. Some of the ways in which you can prepare yourself are to:

- *Research* the organisation/department/directorate – get hold of their annual report and accounts and obtain any information on the area generally.

- *Find out the role of the interviewer(s)* and who else might be involved in the process.

- *Dress smartly* and appropriately.

- *Allow plenty of time for travelling*, including potential delays.

- *Read through the job description/requirements* again. Plan how you will explain any gaps in your knowledge skills and experience – think of skills you have used outside the work environment that can be 'transferred' into the workplace. Take a spare copy of your CV to the interview.

- *Think through what the selection criteria* are likely to be and how you can demonstrate that you have the relevant skills/knowledge/attitude.

- *Prepare questions to ask* and take them with you – it can be difficult to think of questions on the spur of the moment.

- *Prepare answers* to some of the questions provided in the job description or any you dread being asked.

- Review your performance from previous interviews and any practice sessions.

Figure 4.3 presents a checklist for interview preparation.

Figure 4.3 Checklist for interview preparation

	Task	Completed ✓
1	Research the organisation: ■ Key executives ■ Recent developments ■ Service mix ■ Position in market	
2	Research the interviewer(s) or panel members	
3	Plan travel arrangements	
4	Plan what to wear	
5	Make a copy of job description, CV and letter of application	
6	Think through *why* you want this position and what you will contribute to the organisation	
7	Prepare a list of questions to ask	
8	Think through the interviewers' selection criteria – which skills/knowledge/attitudes are they likely to assess?	
9	Think through answers to tricky questions likely to be asked	
10	Decide who to offer as referees and make sure you have spoken to them prior to the interview	

Types of interview

There are several types of interview and you will probably be told in advance what to expect – if not, ask. The three main types of interview are described below.

One-to-one interview

You may have a series of one-to-one interviews with one or more of the following:

- a human resources director/manager;
- a line manager/director;
- a recruitment consultant;
- an occupational psychologist.

Usually the line manager or director will make the final decision, but it is important to impress at *all* stages of the process as you can be rejected at any time. Remember to regard coming in for 'a chat to find out more about the post' as part of the interview process, as although not strictly speaking an interview, the people you meet will form an opinion of you and pass it on.

Panel interview

Panel interviews are the most common form of selection in public sector organisations but not so common in the private sector.

Depending on your level of seniority, the panel might consist of:

- department director;
- a human resources director or manager;

- a consultant/director or manager to whom the post will report;

- an external adviser.

The following considerations apply to panel interviews:

- all candidates are normally interviewed on the same day;

- it tends to be a formal occasion;

- the candidate may be asked to make a presentation on a subject related to the post;

- there is usually a chairperson;

- panel members are usually each responsible for one aspect of the application;

- a decision is often made on the same day.

Remember when answering the questions to make eye contact with *all* panel members (not just the one who is asking the question) and try to give them equal attention.

Assessment centre

Assessment centres are sometimes used for senior management selection and are more common in the private sector. Typically there are several assessors, several candidates, a variety of assessment exercises based on key criteria for the job, and the approach is usually participative. The assessors observe candidates' behaviour throughout individual and group exercises. Typical assessment techniques used are:

- one-to-one interview;
- panel interview;

- group discussion;
- psychometric testing (including aptitude tests and personality questionnaires);
- in-tray exercise (administrative task);
- candidate presentation.

Once they are satisfied with your technical ability, the assessors will test managerial, personal and interpersonal skills. In group sessions, the assessors will observe how you make decisions and solve problems in a team. It is important to use your initiative but also to listen to the views of others.

Do ask to be given feedback about how you have performed; it will give you useful information on how others perceive your strengths and weaknesses. It will also show you are interested in the process.

Apart from preparing for your presentation, unless you are given instructions to do so, you cannot prepare material for an assessment centre other than researching the organisation. It is important to be yourself. Just be aware of the process and try not to compare yourself with the other candidates, as assessment centres are often recruiting for more than one post.

Psychometric tests (including personality questionnaires)

Aptitude tests test your skills in analysis and comprehension. Personality questionnaires assess aspects of personality, which can be relevant to job performance, such as managerial/leadership, thinking and interpersonal skills – there are no right or wrong answers, and they do not assess ability.

Group exercises

In group exercises, assessors observe your behaviour in a group. They will assess both the content of your contribution and how you manage the process.

Following are some general hints to make your behaviour effective:

- Content (what you say)
    - make a positive and enthusiastic contribution;
    - maintain an interested, involved approach;
    - think before speaking;
    - be flexible;
    - practise active listening by observing others and build on their contributions;
    - keep your contributions relevant.
- *Process* (*how* you say it, i.e. the way you behave in group situations)
    - play your part in keeping the discussion on track;
    - encourage quieter members to make contributions;
    - avoid dominance;
    - build on the contributions of others;
    - summarise;
    - manage the time available.

Likely interview questions

Before each interview, it is a good idea to consider the questions you are likely to be asked. You may wish to use this list to prepare for a practice interview. You can then review your answers in preparation for each interview you attend.

Tell me briefly about yourself

- What changes do you see taking place in this post over the next 1/3/5 years?
- What do you perceive to be the problem areas in this job?
- How would your manager/staff/customers describe you?
- What are your main strengths and weaknesses?
- What were your main achievements in your last post?
- What were your main responsibilities in your last post?
- Tell me about your leisure time
- Why should we offer you this post?
- Why have you applied for this post?
- What experience do you bring to this position?
- What other positions have you applied for?
- Where do you see yourself in five years' time?

Difficult/tricky questions

Think carefully how you would respond *positively* to these questions. It is important not to be caught unawares and to remain calm should you feel criticised. These are only examples – there are an infinite number of difficult questions.

- Why do you want to leave your current job?
- What are your weaknesses?
- What salary are you looking for?
- Describe yourself

- Why did you not complete your (library) qualification?
- What would you find difficult in this post?
- What other jobs have you applied for?
- What is your long-term career aim?
- How satisfied are you with your career progression?
- Explain why you have had so many different jobs
- Why should we select you over other candidates?
- Describe your management style
- What were your key priorities in your last job and how were they achieved?
- What was difficult about achieving these priorities?
- Give me an example of where you have managed change in difficult circumstances
- Give me an example of how you have dealt with a difficult colleague/member of staff.

The 'big four' questions

There are four questions which are likely to be asked in an interview, so you may find it helpful to rehearse your response. These are:

- Tell me something about yourself.
- Why are you looking for a new job?
- What would be your ideal role?
- Why have you applied for this post?

For each of these questions, there are some general notes and advice.

Tell me something about yourself

It can be difficult to decide where to start when asked this question. But it is an opportunity for you to 'sell' yourself and concentrate on what you are good at and what you like doing.

You should not talk for too long in response to this question, 5–10 minutes is ample time for a good answer – so time yourself. Try to cover the following:

- The main thread of your experience, e.g. 'I have worked for five years in the bibliographic section and prior to that I was in readers services at EuroLib' or 'I have ten years' literature searching experience in pharmaceutical research'. In addition, articulate what you like about the directorate/department.

- What did you like about the organisations in which you have worked?

- What skills, experience and strengths do you bring to your work?

- A question that involves the interviewer in what you are saying, e.g. 'I could tell you about X or Y. Which would you like me to talk about first?'

- Another approach is to give a brief resumé of your career to date, starting at leaving school/university giving reasons for your career choice and your job changes. This is a structured approach which also gives you the opportunity to sell your skills when you give your reasons for a job change, e.g. 'I moved from ABC company to gain wider experience in X and had the advantage of being able to build on my XYZ skills'.

Whichever approach you decide to take, avoid swamping the interviewer with a mass of information, giving a woolly opening, waffling (i.e. not structuring your response) or finishing in mid-air.

Why are you looking for a new job?

This is a further chance for you to sell yourself if your response is well thought out concise, clear and complete. It is important to remember the following points:

- Think of the positive, 'proactive' reasons you want to move, e.g. career progression, to specialise.

- Do not over-complicate your explanation with too much detail. This can sound like you have something to hide even if you haven't.

- Do not criticise your employer even if you want to move for negative reasons – it is natural to have some negative feelings about any job but they are not relevant to the new post.

What would be your ideal job?

In response to this question, you should cover:

- what you enjoy doing in a job;
- how you like to be able to contribute;
- how you can use your skills, knowledge and experience.

It is easy to be enthusiastic about what you like doing. Describe situations you have enjoyed and projects that have given you personal satisfaction.

Try to link up your preferences with the specific requirements of the job.

Review your CV in terms of your contribution to the organisation; interviewers will be impressed if you express your likes from the point of view of their organisation and how it can benefit them.

Take the opportunity to re-emphasise your skills, but bear in mind the requirement of the particular post you are being interviewed for.

Why have you applied for this post?

In response to this question, you need to prove that:

- the post satisfies most of your goals and aspirations;
- you can match your strengths and achievements to the requirements of the post;
- you feel you could make a contribution to the organisation;
- you are enthusiastic about the organisation and its future.

Each time you attend an interview, you should forget all other applications and put this one at the top of your list. Be honest about your enthusiasm and back it up with facts you have learnt about the organisation. Give examples of your strengths and achievements drawn from your experience.

Questions against specific criteria

Some interviewers will use 'criteria based interviewing'. They will identify the key criteria for effective performance in the job and target their questions against these criteria. There are a host of potential questions against these criteria; some examples below will give you an idea.

- Performance:
  - In this position, how do you define doing a good job?
  - What factors are important to you in judging your subordinates' performance?
  - What tasks do you enjoy at work and why?
- Initiative:
  - Have you had to go against traditions or policies to achieve something? Explain what you did.

- What new ideas or suggestions have you made in the last 12 months?

- How do you get your subordinates to generate new ideas?

- How do you keep technically up-to-date in your field?

■ Pressure:

- Tell me about setbacks you have met and what you did.

- What pressures are there in your job and how do you deal with them?

- What has been the most pressured situation that you have been under recently?

- What are the most demanding aspects of your job?

■ Decision making:

- How do you know when you have got to the bottom of a problem?

- What is the biggest decision you have made in the last year? And what were the alternatives?

- Give me an example of a decision, which, in retrospect, turned out to be wrong? What would you do differently now?

- What methods do you use to make decisions?

- On which decision did you deliberate longest?

■ Innovation:

- What is the most innovative task you have undertaken in your current position?

- What kind of problems have you been called upon to solve?

■ Leadership:

- What groups/committees are you a member of? What is your role and how do you contribute?

- How did you go about setting objectives for your staff last year?

- Give me an example of one of your subordinates with performance problems – what have you done about it?

- Have you ever led a task force or committee or any group that didn't report to you but from whom you have had to get work? How did you go about it? What worked well and what would you do differently in future?

- When do you meet with your immediate subordinates and what is discussed?

■ Interpersonal sensitivity:

- Have you perceived any problems that you have caused others?

- How would you describe your colleagues?

- What was the biggest obstacle you had to overcome to get where you are today? How did you over come it?

■ Flexibility:

- What are the two most different approaches you use in 'selling' ideas?

- What different methods do you use for coping with pressure?

- Describe your most satisfying experience in gaining the support of top management for a proposal

■ Time management:

- How do you schedule your time and set priorities?

- How do you determine the top priorities in your job?

- Tell me how you adjust to sudden pressure being applied.
- Delegation:
  - What type of decision making have you delegated to subordinates?
  - What are your criteria for delegating?
  - How did you keep informed of what was going on? What reports did you use and what controls?
  - How do you like to monitor people working for you?
- Staff development:
  - How do you identify subordinates' needs and potential?
  - Tell me about some of the people who have been successful as a result of your management.
  - How have you helped your subordinates to develop themselves?

Questions you should prepare to ask

Remember you are still being assessed during your questions which, phrased correctly, can demonstrate a real interest and understanding of the organisation. There are numerous areas you could explore but it may be helpful to prepare questions under the following headings:

- future of the organisation (if you are going for an external post);
- mission, values and culture;
- effect of government legislation, company directives and competitors;
- strengths and weaknesses of the department/directorate;
- issues surrounding people in the department (both positive and negative);

- prospects for career progression (speed of promotion, career development and training opportunities);
- responsibilities and objectives for the position over the next 12 months;
- why are you recruiting for this appointment?

The structure of the interview

Interviews will usually follow a pattern, such as this:

- *Step 1*: Introduction – pleasantries, e.g. about your journey, the weather.
- *Step 2*: Interviewer will outline the structure of the meeting.
- *Step 3*: Interviewer will ask you an opening question about yourself or your application, possibly dealing with your most recent employment.
- *Step 4*: Discussions and questions – here the interviewer will test out some or all of the following:
  - *Your attitude* – Are you positive about colleagues/managers?
  - *Your motivation* – How much effort do you give to a job? What interests and challenges you?
  - *Your stability* – How long have you stayed in jobs? Why have you changed jobs? Do you persist in difficult times?
  - *Your maturity* – Do you accept responsibility for your failures? How do you interact with others?
  - *Your aptitudes* – What have you accomplished? What progress have you made? What are your special talents?

- *Your behaviour* – How will you fit in? Are you a team player or do you like to work autonomously? Are you dominant or compliant? Do you work best in an unstructured or structured environment?

■ *Step 5*: Interviewer asks if you have any questions.

■ *Step 6*: Interviewer gives information on terms and conditions.

Managing the interview

You may find it helpful to read through this section before you attend an interview. It should keep you in a positive frame of mind and remind you of what is likely to happen.

■ *Aim to make a good initial impression.* Arrive in plenty of time to allow for a visit to the cloakroom. Ensure you look smart and unruffled by your journey, that your hair is well cut and tidy and your shoes are clean. Tell reception your interview time and who is conducting the interview.

■ *Begin the interview with a firm handshake and/or a friendly greeting.* This means you need to have a hand free, so make sure you transfer your belongings such as your coat and briefcase to your left hand in advance to avoid appearing awkward. You might need to observe cultural customs, so find about these in advance.

■ *Sit down when the interviewer asks you to do so and sit upright without appearing tense.* Do not slouch or fold your arms or put your hands behind your head – non-verbal behaviour can tell the interviewer a great deal about you.

■ *Listen and smile.* You need the interviewer/panel to warm to you, so make it easier for them to do so. Establish eye contact without staring; staring can be threatening.

However, avoiding eye contact altogether can be perceived as representing negative, shifty or nervous behaviour.

- *Pick up non-verbal signals from the interviewer.* Nods and 'Yes, good' mean 'do continue'. A tapping pen and interruptions mean 'I've had enough'.

- *Think before you speak.* It is preferable to be silent for a while rather than rushing your response. This will give you time to give a measured, reasoned and positive answer. State your views and opinions with confidence. If you disagree with the interviewer's views, do not say so.

- *Do not interrupt the interviewer.* If they are verbose (this is unlikely to happen in panel interviews as the chairperson manages the time) and do not give you the opportunity to present the convincing argument you prepared, try to make each contribution extremely positive.

- *Answer the question that is asked.* Do not answer the question that you would like to have been asked. However, it is quite acceptable to then turn the question to your advantage. Take every opportunity to show that you can solve problems, particularly those in the job in question.

- *Answer the question precisely and succinctly.* Then offer to elaborate further if required or turn the question back on the interviewer to appear interested in their viewpoint.

- *Show the interviewer that you have researched the organisation.* Ask relevant questions or relating your experience and skills to the needs of the service.

- *Do not lie or exaggerate about anything.* You are likely to be found out, particularly if you are asked to expand upon your claim. The interviewer may know more about you than you realise, e.g. references, checks.

- *If asked about your salary expectations, give a reasonable response.* Keep your response in line with the advertised salary and your current salary.

- *If the salary on offer is significantly higher than your current salary, you should have good reasons why you qualify for a substantial increase.* You need to consider the complete package as well as the basic salary – while the salary on offer may appear low, the package might substantially increase its value (e.g. pension).

Now think through your responses to the questions you are likely to be asked. Why do you want this position? Why are you the right person for the post? And why should we give it to you?

The interviewer will want to know how you will tackle this job. They will hope you are the person for the job; prove to them that you are.

Meeting subordinates/fellow team members

You may be invited to meet other people who you would work with. These meetings may not be described as 'interviews' and may not seem like interviews, but you should assume you are being assessed nonetheless. Before a meeting, always find out what you can about the people you are going to meet.

For managerial positions, it is likely you will be asked to meet some or all of your subordinate team. Remember that interviews are two-way and that this is an opportunity for you to assess whether you would like to work with this team.

Potential subordinates are unlikely to interview you but they will of course form judgments about what you say. It may be useful to discuss how they see the future priorities for the team/department/organisation and then assess whether these match your views/values.

Areas for discussion could be:

- the individual's experience and background;
- how they view their job and priorities;
- any particular difficulties;
- goals for the coming year.

Areas to avoid include:

- their views of their current manager or the ultimate director/manager of the department;
- telling them about yourself (unless they ask and then keep it brief);
- implying you know very little and need information from them;
- implying you know everything.

Even if you are not asked to meet members of the team, it may be worth requesting meetings, especially to learn more about the values and culture of the organisation (if you are looking for a position outside your organisation); such requests are usually well received.

Closing interview

Always try to conclude the interview on a positive note. Thank the interviewer for their time and interest in your application and refer to any aspect of the job or organisation that particularly impressed you. Always ask a final question of the interviewer, such as what is the next stage in the selection process?

5

Learning styles

Introduction

'Learning is your most important capability simply because it is the gateway to every other capability you might wish to develop' (Honey and Mumford, 2006). People who are actively involved in their own learning process feel more empowered, which increases their chance of success and personal achievement.

Table 5.1 presents motivations for and barriers to learning. Successful outcomes of learning include:

- people feel more responsibility for something they have helped to create;
- commitment to completing a given task and reaching a desired outcome;
- being steered in the right direction;
- effectively utilising skills, experience and expertise;
- feeling of comfort;
- feeling of achievement or satisfaction;
- improved performance and productivity;
- self-development, improved learning;
- improved relationship;
- improved quality of life in the workplace;

| Table 5.1 | Motivations for and barriers to learning |

Motivation	Barriers
Make or maintain social relationships	Other responsibilities
Meet external expectations	Lack of time or money
Learn to serve others better	Lack of resources or facilities
Professional advancement	Timetabling problems
Escape or stimulation	Transportation problems
Pure interest	Lack of confidence, fear of ignorance
Opportunity	Not interested or ready to learn
Gap in learning	Forced to learn

- better use of people, time and resources;
- more creativity;
- more flexibility and adaptability to change.

The learning process is completed on three levels:

- *cognition*: how one acquires knowledge;
- *conceptualisation*: how one processes information;
- *affective*: individual's motivation, decision-making styles, values and emotional preferences.

A key ingredient of the learning process is understanding how we learn and identifying our preferred style of learning. 'Being aware of your preferred learning style is now widely acknowledged as a prerequisite to becoming a better all-round learner' (Honey and Mumford, 2006). A number of learning styles instruments have been developed that help to identify personal preferences and a selection of these are reviewed in this chapter.

Adult learning

> *Pedagogy*: The science of teaching; instruction, training. Origin: Greek *Paidagogs*: a slave who led a boy to school [*Pados* boy, *Agein* to lead, and *à agogos* leader] (*Chambers Dictionary*, 1994)

Learning, training and education are normally seen as pedagogical activities, that is teacher-focused education for children. However, there is a view that adults' approach to learning differs from the way children are taught. The notion of andragogy has been around for nearly two centuries, falling in and out of favour. It became particularly popular in North America and Britain as a way of describing adult learning.

Andragogy and the name of Malcolm Knowles have become inextricably linked. For Knowles, andragogy was defined on four crucial assumptions about the characteristics of adult learners. A fifth was added later:

- *Self-concept*: As a person matures, their self-concept moves from being a dependent personality toward being a self-directed human being.

- *Experience*: As a person matures, they accumulate a growing reservoir of experience that becomes an increasing resource for learning.

- *Readiness to learn*: As a person matures, their readiness to learn becomes orientated to the developmental tasks of their social roles.

- *Orientation to learning*: As a person matures, their time perspective changes from postponed application of knowledge to immediacy of application, and accordingly their orientation toward learning shifts from subject-centeredness to problem centeredness.

- *Motivation to learn*: As a person matures, the motivation to learn is internal (Knowles, 1984: 12).

Critical thinking

According to Bloom (1956), learning takes place at six levels (see Figure 5.1). At each level, the questions asked are intended to increase competence, skills and critical thinking. The ability to ask the right question at the right level to determine a user enquiry is fundamental to the information profession.

In terms of higher order questioning, critical thinking can broken down as follows:

- *inquisitiveness*: curiosity;

- *open-mindedness*: tolerant, divergent;

- *systematic*: orderly, organised;

- *analytical*: reasoning, evidence;

- *truth seeking*: best knowledge;

- *self-confidence*: judgment, rational;

- *maturity*: approach to problems.

Figure 5.1   Bloom's taxonomy (hierarchy of learning)

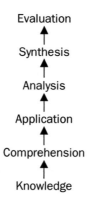

Evaluation

Synthesis

Analysis

Application

Comprehension

Knowledge

In terms of curricula:

- Critical skills are essential for lifelong learning.
- Instead of providing knowledge, the curricula should challenge students to strive for critical scientific thinking, solving problems and communicating with the user.
- The goals of critical thinking are to assess the credibility of information and to work through problems the best way.
- Imposing factual information and learning on students does not foster reasoning.
- Effective trainers facilitate the development of critical-thinking skills when they implement learning activities that have authentic, real-world contexts and personal relevance to the students.
- Well-designed, open-ended questions and investigative activities by the trainer facilitate thinking.
- Trainers, in general, ask significantly lower-level cognitive questions than higher-level questions.
- Questions should be designed to promote evaluation and synthesis of facts and concepts.

Table 5.2 presents Bloom's taxonomy in terms of competence, skills demonstrated and questions.

Learning styles

There are a number of diagnostic instruments available to help identify the individual's preferred learning style. These instruments normally take the form of self-assessment questionnaires. Although examples of these questionnaires may be found on the Internet, many of the learning style instruments are copyright or need a licence. However, it is

Table 5.2   Bloom's taxonomy

Competence	Skills demonstrated	Questions
Knowledge: Knowing terminology, specific facts, ways and means of dealing with specifics (conventions, trends and sequences, classifications and categories, criteria, methodology), universals and abstractions in a field (principles and generalisations, theories and structures); remembering (recalling) appropriate, previously learned information	Observation and recall of information Knowledge of dates, events, places Knowledge of major ideas Mastery of subject matter	collect, define, describe, enumerate, examine, identify, label, list match, name, quote, read, record, reproduce, select, show, state, tabulate, tell, view, who, when, where
Comprehension: Grasping (understanding) the meaning of informational materials	Understanding information Grasp meaning Translate knowledge into new context Interpret facts, compare, contrast Order, group, infer causes Predict consequences	associate, classify, cite, contrast, convert, describe, differentiate, discuss, distinguish, estimate, explain, extend, generalise, give examples, interpret, make sense out of, paraphrase, predict, restate in own words, summarise, trace, understand
Application: The use of previously learned information in new and concrete situations to solve problems that have single or best answers	Use information Use methods, concepts, theories in new situations Solve problems using required skills or knowledge	act, administer, apply articulate, assess, calculate, change, chart, collect, complete, compute, construct, contribute, control, demonstrate, determine, develop, discover, establish,

Table 5.2   Bloom's taxonomy (*Cont'd*)

		examine, experiment, extend, illustrate, implement, include, inform, instruct, modify, participate, predict, prepare, preserve, produce, project, provide, relate, report, show, solve, teach, transfer, use, utilise
Analysis: The breaking down of informational materials into their component parts, examining (and trying to understand the organisational structure of) such information to develop divergent conclusions by identifying motives or causes, making inferences, and/or finding evidence to support generalisations	Analysis, seeing patterns Organisation of parts Recognition of hidden meanings Identification of components	analyse, arrange, break down, compare, connect, correlate, differentiate, discriminate, distinguish, divide, explain, focus, illustrate, infer, limit, order, outline, point out, prioritise, recognise, select, separate, subdivide
Synthesis: Creatively or divergently applying prior knowledge and skills to produce a new or original whole	Use old ideas to create new ones Generalise from given facts Relate knowledge from several areas Predict, draw conclusions	adapt, anticipate, categorise, collaborate, combine, communicate, compare, compile, compose, contrast, create, design, devise, express, facilitate, formulate, generate, incorporate, initiate, integrate, intervene, invent, model, modify, negotiate, plan, prepare, progress, rearrange, reconstruct, reinforce, reorganise,

Table 5.2   Bloom's taxonomy (*Cont'd*)

		revise, rewrite, structure, substitute, validate, what if?
Evaluation: Judging the value of material based on personal values/opinions, resulting in an end-product with a given purpose, without real right or wrong answers	Compare and discriminate between ideas Assess value of theories, presentations Make choices based on reasoned argument Verify value of evidence Recognise subjectivity	appraise, assess, compare and contrast, conclude, convince, criticise, critique, decide, defend, explain, grade, interpret, judge, justify, measure, recommend, reframe, rank, select, summarise, support, test

still possible for a person to identify with the characteristics of the learning style without completing the questionnaire. It is noted that some countries/cultures favour one approach or instrument over another.

A learning style is a unique collection of individual skills and preferences that affect how a person perceives, gathers and processes information. The idea is to use the learner's preferred style as a starting point, and then reinforce the learning with other styles. Styles can expand as learners become more adept. Although each person has a preferred style, they will embrace all elements of the style at some stage. For instance, the reflective learner will need to take a more active approach at some point. Visual learners will benefit from auditory and kinaesthetic experiences as well. The learning styles may show a strong, moderate or mild preference towards one or more elements.

This chapter considers the following learning style theories:

- Jung type indicators;
- Auditory, visual, kinaesthetic;

- Multiple intelligences;
- Kolb;
- Honey Mumford.

A brief description of the diagnostic instruments of the learning styles theories is given below.

Jung indicators applied to learning

Jung indicators are based on his personality theory, later expanded using diagnostic instruments, such as the Myers Briggs Type Indicator (MBTI), to reflect preferred learning styles. A number of learning inventories have been developed that use Jungian dimensions to identify preferred styles, such as Pelley, and the Paragon Learning Style Inventory (PLSI). According to Jung a person is:

- extrovert (E) or introvert (I);
- sensing (S) or intuition (N);
- thinking (T) or feeling (F);
- judging (J) or perceiving (P).

Table 5.3 expands on the descriptions of these learning styles. Combined, these translate to 16 types of learning style (ESTP, ESFP, ENFP, ENTP, ESTJ, ESFJ, ENFJ, ENTJ, ISTJ, ISFJ, INFJ, INTJ, ISTP, ISFP, INFP and INTP), each with defining characteristics.

Auditory, visual, kinaesthetic (tactile) learning

The auditory, visual, kinaesthetic (AVK) learning style has enjoyed a re-emergence as a learning style. It is reckoned

Table 5.3   Jung type learning styles

Extrovert (E)	Introvert (I)
People and things	Concepts, ideas, abstraction, thinker
Interaction with other people	Tranquillity
Action-oriented, think on their feet	Reflective
Talk more than listen	Think rather than talk
Learn by teaching others (need to explain to others in order to understand themselves)	Develop frameworks that connect information, turning it into knowledge
Problem-based learning in groups	
Sensing (S)	**Intuition (N)**
Rely on their five senses	Hunches and sixth sense
Detail-oriented, wanting facts	Look for big picture (metaphor and analogies)
Prefer organisational, linear and structured learning	Imagination and innovation
Systematic step-by-step approach	Like to compare and contrast (concept map)
Thinking (T)	**Feeling (F)**
Impersonal-based analysis, logic principles and objective criteria	Value harmony and empathy
Value fairness and situation logic	Focus on human values which they need to make valued decisions and judgments
Place weight on objective criteria	
Critical, seeing flaws	Able to facilitate differences among groups members; power of persuasion
Prefer clear goals and objectives	
Want to know what they have to do to learn	Enjoy small (harmonious) group exercises
Judging (J)	**Perceiving (P)**
Decisive, self-starters, self-improvement, planners and self-regimented	Curious, adaptable and spontaneous, last minute
Take action quickly	Start tasks, want to know everything about task, do not always complete the task
Focus on essentials of task and completing the task	
Deadlines are sacred and time a finite resource	Deadlines are stretched
	Time is a renewable resource
Need tools to help them plan work activities; quick tip guides	Options are left open
	Postpone or defer actions to the last minute
Should be encouraged by offering self-improvement opportunities	Process oriented
	Complex projects need to be broken into smaller assignments

| Table 5.4 | Auditory, visual, kinaesthetic learning styles |

Auditory: Hear – Learns best by using their ears and their voices
Talks to him/herself, reads aloud
Sometimes has difficulty reading and writing
Often does better by talking to colleagues
Often effective speakers
Remembers what they hear and their own verbal expressions
Remembers by talking aloud and through verbal repetition
Prefers to talk through a concept not understood
Verbally expressed excitement about learning
Can remember verbal instructions without recording them
Enjoys discussions and talking with others
Easily distracted by sound and silence
Enjoys interesting lessons
Finds it difficult to work quietly for extended periods of time
Enjoys music activities

Visual: See – Learns best by using their eyes
Two subchannels – linguistic and spatial
Visual-spatial – videos, demonstrations
Prefers to see words written down; taking and making notes
Imagines pictures of something being described
Prefers time to remember historical events
Prefers written instructions for assignments
Observes all the physical elements in a classroom
Carefully organises their learning materials
Enjoys decorating learning areas and visual art activities
Prefers photography and illustrations with printed content
Remembers and understands through the use of diagrams, charts and maps
Appreciates presentations using slides, handouts
Studies materials by reading over notes and organising in outline form

Kinaesthetic: Do – Learns best by using their hands
May appear 'slow' to learn
Loss of concentration if little movement or external stimulation
Doodles, uses highlighters, colour codes
Two subchannels – movement and touch (tactile)
Becomes physically involved in the subject being studied
Enjoys acting out a situation
Prefers making a product or completing a project
Prefers building and physically handling learning materials
Remembers and understands through doing something
Takes study notes to keep busy but often does not need them
Enjoys using computers
Physically expresses enthusiasm by getting active and excited
Finds it difficult to sit still for extended periods of time
Enjoys hands-on activities

that 30 per cent of the population learn best by hearing, talking and verbal expression, with 65 per cent of the population preferring visual learning through seeing, observing and pictorial image. The remaining 5 per cent are kinaesthetic or tactile learners who understanding by doing, touching and hands-on experience. These learning styles are summarised in Table 5.4.

Multiple Intelligence Inventory

In 1983, Dr Howard Gardner, professor of education at Harvard University, developed the Multiple Intelligence Inventory (MII) model. He suggested that the traditional notion of intelligence, based on intelligence quotient (IQ) testing, was flawed and limited. The MII defines eight styles of learning, summarised in Table 5.5. In many ways, MII resembles AVK but breaks down each category into more detailed groupings.

Kolb concepts

David Kolb was one of the first to approach learning style from the educational rather than psychoanalytical perspective. Although Kolb's model is used extensively around the world, many people find it difficult to understand as it uses vague wording and is based on self-perception. Kolb's do, reflect, interpret, plan (DRIP) learning cycle refers to the processes by which individuals understand their experiences and modify their behaviours. The logic of this learning cycle model is to 'learn by doing' and then using reflective practice to make small incremental improvements. The cycle helps to realise strengths and understand weaknesses.

| Table 5.5 | Multiple Intelligence Inventory learning style | |

Learner category	Traits	Learns best by
Linguistic (word)	Likes to read, write and tell stories, enjoys trivia	saying, hearing and seeing words
Logical/mathematical (number/reasoning)	Likes to do experiments, figure things out, work with numbers, good at logic, reasoning and problem solving	categorising, classifying and working with abstract patterns/relationships
Spatial (picture)	Likes to draw, build, design and create things, daydream; is good at imagining things, sensing changes, mazes/puzzles and reading maps, charts	visualising, dreaming, using the mind's eye and working with colours/pictures
Musical (music)	Likes to sing, listen to music, play an instrument and respond to music, is good at remembering melodies and keeping time	rhythm, melody and music
Bodily/kinaesthetic (body)	Likes to move around, touch and talk and use body language; is good at physical activities such as sport, dance and crafts	touching, moving, interacting with space and processing knowledge through bodily sensations
Naturalistic (nature)	Likes to be outside, with animals, geography, and weather; interacting with the surroundings; environment and conservation	studying nature, working in a natural setting, learning about how things work
Interpersonal (people)	Likes to have lots of friends, talk to people and join groups, mediation skills	sharing, comparing, relating, cooperating and interviewing

Table 5.5	Multiple Intelligence Inventory learning style (*Cont'd*)	
Intrapersonal (self)	Likes to work alone and pursue own interests, focusing inward on feelings, following instincts, pursuing own interests	working alone, singleton projects, self-paced instruction and having own space

The four axes of the learning cycle are described below, and summarised in Table 5.6.

Concrete experience (CE) – doing

This focuses on being involved in experiences and dealing with immediate human situations in a personal way. It emphasises feelings as opposed to thinking. CE people gather experience by 'living the experience'.

People with CE orientation:

- are good at relating to others;
- have an open-minded approach to life;
- enjoy being involved in real situations;
- enjoy being involved in new experiences.

Reflective observation (RO) – reflecting

This focuses on understanding the meaning of ideas and situations by carefully observing them and impartially describing them. It emphasises understanding as opposed to practical application. RO people tend to think about experiences and reflect upon them.

Table 5.6 **Kolb learning types**

Concrete experience		
	Type 4: Accommodators (sensing) Concrete experience/active experimenter accommodators are active learners who are encouraged by independent discovery. They are generally good with complex situations and relationships. Accommodators ask 'what if' questions like 'what would happen if I did this?'	Type 1: Divergers (feeling) Concrete experience/ reflective observer divergers prefer to have information presented to them in a detailed, systematic and reasoned manner. They like to explore what a system has to offer. Divergers ask 'why' questions like 'why did this happen?'
Active experimentation	Type 3: Convergers (thinking) Abstract conceptualisation/ active experimenter convergers like interaction rather than passive activity. By understanding detailed information about a system's operation they are able to increase the application and usefulness of information. Convergers ask 'how' questions like 'how has this come about?'	Type 2: Assimilators (introvert) Abstract conceptualisation/ reflective observer assimilators like to get the 'right' answer to the problem in an orderly way based on accurate information. They have respect for the knowledgeable expert. Assimilators ask 'what' questions like 'what is there to know?'
Abstract conceptualisation		

(right side label: Reflective observation)

People with RO orientation:

- enjoy defining the meaning of situations and ideas;
- are good at looking at things from different perspectives or viewpoints;
- rely on their own thoughts and feelings to form opinions;
- value patience, impartiality, consideration and thoughtful judgment;
- watch others, and experience through seeing.

Abstract conceptualisation (AC) – interpreting

This focuses on using logic, ideas and concepts. It emphasises thinking as opposed to feeling. AC people are likely to use a scientific rather than an artistic approach.

People with AC orientation:

- are good at systematic planning and quantitative analysis;
- value precision, rigour and discipline and the aesthetic quality of a neat conceptual system;
- create theories to explain observations;
- use second-hand information – experience by being told about it.

Abstract experimentation (AE) – planning

This focuses on actively influencing people and changing situations. It emphasises practical applications as opposed to reflective understanding, doing as opposed to observing. AE people like using theories to solve problems and make decisions.

People with AE orientation:

- are good at getting things accomplished;
- are willing to take risks in order to achieve goals;
- enjoy having influence on the environment around them and like to see results;
- having grasped the experience, will investigate further in an active way.

People have to experience each aspect of the learning cycle but have a tendency toward particular learning styles. The preferred learning styles are then summed up as four types (Table 5.6):

- divergers;

- assimilators;

- convergers;

- accommodators.

Honey Mumford

The Honey Mumford model of learning styles bears great similarity to Kolb's concept of doers and thinkers. This model is widely used throughout the world. The four stages of the learning cycle are mutually supportive and equally important (see Figure 5.2). Each person possesses the characteristics of each style but has a preference towards one or two styles, for example, reflector/theorist or activist/pragmatist. Table 5.7 gives a breakdown of the characteristics of each style.

Figure 5.2   **Honey Mumford Learning Cycle**

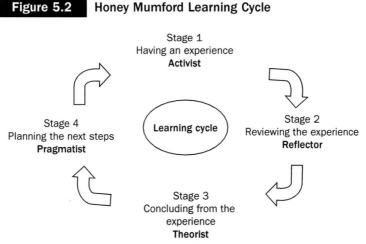

Stage 1
Having an experience
Activist

Stage 4
Planning the next steps
Pragmatist

Learning cycle

Stage 2
Reviewing the experience
Reflector

Stage 3
Concluding from the experience
Theorist

© Honey, P. and Mumford, A. (2006) *The Learning Styles Questionnaire 80-item version*, p. 5

| Table 5.7 | Honey Mumford learning types |

Doers	Thinkers
Activists: Do – Experience Activists will immerse themselves fully in new experiences. They tend to act first, consider consequences later. They are enthusiastic gregarious people who want to be the centre of activity. They thrive on the challenge of new experiences, but are bored with implementation. Activists' approach is 'I'll try anything once'.	Reflectors: Think – Review Reflectors prefer to stand back and observe. They are good listeners. They like to collect and assimilate data before coming to any conclusions. They are cautious and adopt a low profile, sometimes seeming rather remote or distant. They do not like to be rushed and may seem slow to respond. Reflectors' approach is I'll think about it'.
Pragmatists: Do – Plan Pragmatists are practical down-to-earth people who are keen to put ideas, theories and techniques into practice. They act quickly and confidently on ideas, getting straight to the point. They are impatient with digressions, irrelevancies and endless discussion. Pragmatists' approach is 'I know there is always a better way'.	Theorists: Think – Conclude Theorists think through problems in a logical manner, value rationality and objectivity but are uncomfortable with subjective judgments. They assimilate disparate facts into coherent theories. They tend to be perfectionists and may seem to be detached. Theorists' approach is 'Does it make sense?'

Conclusion

Adults possess a combination of intelligence strengths and learning styles. Each person learns in a different way and has a unique style of gathering, processing and interpreting information. A mismatch between the learning style and the way educative material is presented may result in the individual being less effective, loss of motivation and giving up on the learning activity. Knowing about your own learning style will help you to be more motivated about your learning activity. It will also help to develop coping strategies to deal with areas perceived as weaknesses.

The people who you train may learn in a different way to you. As such, you will need to vary your instructional techniques to use methods that help to promote learning among your trainees, for example, staff, users. This means that they will respond more positively to a learning activity in which you, the trainer, incorporate one or more areas of their learning styles.

6

Developing courses

This chapter reviews the main elements that should be considered when developing a course, whether this is setting objectives, defining the course content or equipment needs, or identifying a suitable venue. The first section of the chapter uses a systematic approach to planning to identify the needs, aims, objectives, methods, implementation and evaluation. The second section reviews administrative arrangements, selecting trainers and developing courseware. The third section provides a listing of the more popular training methods. The fourth section gives a list of equipment together with points for consideration, such as troubleshooting.

Systematic approach to planning a training event

Defining the need

The first point is to establish the training need:

- the topic, e.g. searching skills, thesaurus construction, supervisory skills;

- the level, e.g. beginner, intermediate, advanced;

- the audience, e.g. LIS staff, managers, specialists (doctors, engineers).

Defining the audience

In reviewing the audience needs, a number of questions must be clarified at the outset. These include the depth of knowledge to be imparted (what does the audience need to know?), and the ability, experience and expertise of the potential participants. An audience of mixed ability means that the course will be directed at the lowest level or least experienced. There are various ways in which the level can be determined, from self-assessment questionnaires, appraisals and interviews to observation and well-defined course descriptors. The next question relates to the time – how long will the training take to complete and how much time do they have – 20 minutes, two hours, all day? This will determine the depth, pace and length of the training. For some people, the training may be progressive, that is increasing in level and complexity, from beginner to advanced.

Other influencing factors include the number of people attending the course or training session:

- one or two people, e.g. one-to-one;
- small group, e.g. 5–10 people;
- large group, e.g. 20 or more people.

Another area for consideration is the attention given to special needs such as

- visual impairment;
- hearing impairment;
- wheelchair access;
- literacy/numeracy skills.

The main elements to consider when designing a training programme are presented in Figure 6.1.

Figure 6.1 Designing a training programme – main elements

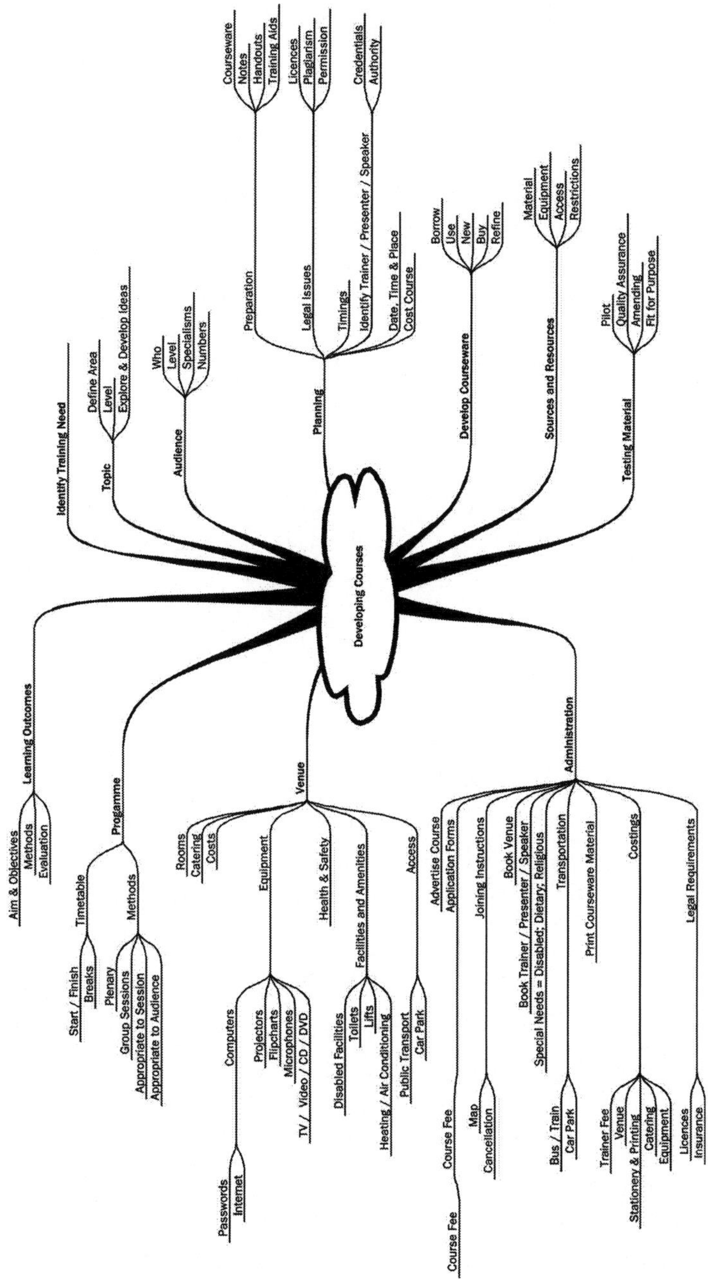

Developing Courses

Identify Training Need
- Topic
  - Define Area
  - Level
  - Explore & Develop Ideas
- Audience
  - Who
  - Level
  - Specialisms
  - Numbers

Planning
- Preparation
  - Courseware
    - Notes
    - Handouts
    - Training Aids
- Legal Issues
  - Licences
  - Plagiarism
  - Permission
  - Credentials
  - Authority
- Timings
  - Identify Trainer / Presenter / Speaker
  - Date, Time & Place
  - Cost Course

Develop Courseware
- Borrow
- Use
- New
- Buy
- Refine

Sources and Resources
- Material
- Equipment
- Access
- Restrictions

Testing Material
- Pilot
- Quality Assurance
- Amending
- Fit for Purpose

Learning Outcomes
- Aim & Objectives
- Methods
- Evaluation

Programme
- Timetable
  - Start / Finish
  - Breaks
  - Plenary
- Methods
  - Group Sessions
  - Appropriate to Session
  - Appropriate to Audience

Venue
- Rooms
- Catering
- Costs
- Equipment
  - Computers
    - Passwords
    - Internet
  - Projectors
  - Flipcharts
  - Microphones
  - TV / Video / CD / DVD
- Health & Safety
- Facilities and Amenities
  - Disabled Facilities
  - Toilets
  - Lifts
  - Heating / Air Conditioning
  - Public Transport
  - Car Park
- Access

Administration
- Advertise Course
- Application Forms
- Joining Instructions
  - Course Fee
  - Map
  - Cancellation
- Book Venue
- Book Trainer / Presenter / Speaker
- Special Needs = Disabled; Dietary; Religious
- Transportation
  - Bus / Train
  - Car Park
- Print Courseware Material
- Costings
  - Course Fee
  - Trainer Fee
  - Venue
  - Stationery & Printing
  - Catering
  - Equipment
  - Licences
  - Insurance
- Legal Requirements

Aim and objectives

This section uses the words 'aim' and 'objectives', but recognises that other terms are often used, such as purpose, goals or targets.

A course will have one aim but a number of objectives. An aim has three parts:

- intention (... is to ...)
- provision (... in order to ...)
- outcome (... so that ...)

Thus, for example:

> The aim *is to* raise awareness of the key principles of financial management *in order to* provide sound foundations for the development of book-keeping and accountancy skills *so that* effective library accounts and ledgers are maintained.

The objectives define what the training will endeavour to achieve. Use the SMART acronym (specific/stretching, measurable, achievable/agreed, realistic, time-bound) when setting objectives, with a limit of 3–7 objectives per course. In addition to being SMART, Whitmore (1992) suggests that objectives should be PURE (positively stated, understood, relevant, ethical) and CLEAR (challenging, legal, environmentally sound, agreed, recorded).

Wherever possible objectives should be active (create, produce, build) rather than passive (discuss, examine, list), as these are easier to measure.

A useful way to write objectives is to use the phase 'at the end of the course (session, workshop) the participants will have...' and then identify the objectives for the course. For example:

At the end of the course, participants will have:

- structured a search strategy using a variety of tools and operators;
- refined a search strategy to expand or reduce the number of hits retrieved;
- used different search engines and know their limitations;
- identified and bookmarked authoritative sites for future reference;
- navigated the World Wide Web to locate specific data.

Learning outcomes are derived from the objectives. So what would you expect them to know at the end of the training and how are you going to measure the learning?

Methods

How will the objectives be achieved? Will there be a plenary to introduce the topic followed by a brainstorming session or buzz groups? Will you use questionnaires or other diagnostic instruments? Will the participants be working on their own or in small groups? Select the method that will maximise on the output and achieve the objective. A selection of training methods is listed in this chapter.

Implement

When putting the objectives and methods into practice, it is worth remembering that all training sessions vary and that a method successfully used on one course will not produce the same result on another. Trainers should try experimenting with a number of different approaches. Summarise what you have done so far and check for understanding. Make sure that your audience knows each time you begin a new part of the programme.

It is not always necessary to have feedback at the end of each segment of the programme, but let your participants know if they are expected to feed back the results of their discussion or findings. Only use feedback if it adds value to the training session.

When running training courses it is important to remember that people learn in different ways and the pace will vary according to the make-up of the audience. There are no 'rights' or 'wrongs'. Each person has a preferred learning style(s) that may not accord with the trainer's presentation technique. In some cases opposite styles can lead to tension and conflict.

Part of the implementation phase will be to ensure that all equipment is in place and working. An action plan should be held in reserve in case of an emergency. All trainers can relate horror stories of equipment failure. Presenters have been known to put their material on the Internet, only to find a lack of connectivity, with no alternative arrangements having been made. A list of equipment and some thoughts about usage are given at the end of this chapter.

Evaluation

At the end of the training, the course must be evaluated by both participants and the trainer and/or course organiser. Table 6.1 presents an example of how a trainer might evaluate a course. Examples of blank participant course evaluation forms are given in Tables 6.2 and 6.3.

A tool used to evaluate the course should review it from the planning stage to delivery outcome. It should assess the relevance of the content, methods and process by reflecting on what has gone well and what difficulties occurred, why

| Table 6.1 | Director's end of course evaluation form |

What went well?	Why?	Future action plan
Admin		
Central Hall (Venue) and rooms	Central location well served by public transport	Use Central Hall (venue) for future training
Everyone arrived on time	Joining instructions gave adequate details about venue and public transport	Send out joining instructions in plenty of time with map and other details
Participants		
Content	Keen willing and enthusiastic group	Encourage participants to contribute to each session
Overall well balanced programme	Clear objectives that addressed learning needs	Retain programme with practical session running after lunch
Practical afternoon session very well received	Hands-on putting theory of morning to use	Test learning and understanding throughout day
Methods		
Case studies and practical demonstration particularly effective	Methods enhanced understanding	Use methods appropriate to session
What difficulties occurred?	**Why?**	**Future action plan**
Admin		
Catering – refreshments	No tea, coffee or biscuits on arrival	Confirm catering arrangements three days before course
Catering – lunch	No vegetarian option at lunch	Ensure dietary needs are catered for
Content		
Disruption to session 2	Fire alarm – evacuated building for 30 minutes	Ensure programme has in-built flexibility to allow for disruptions
Methods		
Building a mind map	Needed to explain method, adding	Ensure participants are familiar with methods used

Table 6.1 Director's end of course evaluation form (*Cont'd*)

	extra ten minutes to session	and that clear explanation is given at outset
Feedback at end of session 3	Overran, not clear what was wanted and too much detail	Clarify what is wanted from feedback and how it should be presented

Overall success of course
Comments from evaluation indicated that course was well received and pitched at right level.
Staff helpful at venue as there had been confusion over the catering arrangements.
More flexibility needs to be built into future courses. Need to review the use of feedback and have example of how to build a mind map.

Table 6.2 Participant evaluation form (1)

Please take a few minutes to give us some feedback by completing this evaluation form. Your comments will help shape the future of other courses and presentations.

On a scale of 1–5 (1 = poor; 5 = excellent) please indicate your opinion of:

Course	Poor		Good		Excellent		Use again	
The programme as a whole	1	2	3	4	5	6	Yes	No
Content	1	2	3	4	5	6	Yes	No
Format	1	2	3	4	5	6	Yes	No
Joining instructions	1	2	3	4	5	6	Yes	No
Information given out before the course	1	2	3	4	5	6	Yes	No
Information given out during the course	1	2	3	4	5	6	Yes	No
Venue	1	2	3	4	5	6	Yes	No
Catering	1	2	3	4	5	6	Yes	No

What learning did you gain from this session?

What, in your opinion, were the strengths of this course?

What, in your opinion, were the weaknesses of this course?

What changes, if any, should be made to the course?

Other comments:

Thank you for your help.

Table 6.3   Participant evaluation form (2)

Course title:
Level:
Course date:
Venue:
Tutor/facilitator:

		Poor	Good	Very good	Excellent
1	How well did the course programme meet the stated objectives?	1	2	3	4
2	How well did it match your own learning needs?	1	2	3	4
3	How interesting did you find it?	1	2	3	4
4	How relevant did you find it?	1	2	3	4
5	How would you rate the design of today's programme?	1	2	3	4
6	How would you rate the style of the tutors/facilitators?	1	2	3	4
7	How would you rate the knowledge of the tutors/facilitators	1	2	3	4
8	How would you rate the pace of the day?	1	2	3	4
9	How would you rate the different learning approaches used during the day (e.g. small groups, exercises)	1	2	3	4
10	How valuable was it to learn with other colleagues?	1	2	3	4
11	How would you rate your overall level of satisfaction with the course programme?	1	2	3	4
12	How useful did you find the opportunity to reflect on the day?	1	2	3	4

Table 6.3	Participant evaluation form (2) (*Cont'd*)

13	Do you believe that course is likely to have an impact on your future practice?	Yes	No
14	Would you recommend this course to a colleague?	Yes	No
15	What could be done to improve the course?		
16	Are there any other comments you would like to make?		

Thank you very much for your help and cooperation in completing this evaluation.

Adapted from Managing Life in the NHS.

they produced such results and what should happen in the future. The latter forms the future action plan and contributes to succession planning.

The section on difficulties should include obstacles or other external influences that hindered or affected the success of the training, such as transportation problems, power failure, non-compatibility of equipment.

Courses need to be constantly evolving as situations change. The outcome of the evaluation influences how the course should be developed and delivered in the future. Acting on the evaluation ensures that the courses stay fit for purpose and do not stagnate.

Administrative arrangements

Timetable for arrangements

Having decided to run a course, it is important to know whether or not the event will go ahead. This will be influenced by costs, numbers, suitable venue and availability of trainer or speakers. Mechanisms must be in place if a course is to be changed, cancelled or deferred so that all parties are kept aware of the situation.

A number of steps need to be completed prior to running a course, from booking the venue and sorting out equipment, to placing the advertisement, sending out the joining instructions and briefing the trainer. A brief outline of these functions is given below and templates or examples are included where appropriate.

Advertising the course

The intention to run a course needs to be advertised at suitable locations. This notification could be circulated via the Web, placed on noticeboards, mentioned in journals, listed in training directories, posted on mailing lists or sent direct to targeted groups. Details posted should be sufficient for an individual to make an informed decision as to the suitability of the course to meet personal needs, or a contact point given for further information to be provided.

Course advertisement details should include the following:

- sponsoring organisation;
- title and level;
- date, time, venue;
- trainers or presenters;
- course outline (e.g. purpose, sessions, learning outcomes);
- target group (e.g. library assistants, supervisors);
- numbers (e.g. maximum 15 participants);
- booking or reservation procedures (e.g. application forms, closing date);

- course fee;
- cancellation;
- contact details (e.g. telephone number, e-mail address).

Application form details should include the following:

- name and address of applicant;
- contact details (telephone, fax number, e-mail);
- membership details if appropriate;
- position/job title;
- organisation;
- course title and course date;
- course location;
- course fee;
- cancellation fee (e.g. 10 per cent deposit or non-refundable fee details);
- method of payment (e.g. cheque/debit card/invoice);
- details of who to return the form to (contact name, address, telephone, fax number, e-mail).

A sample application form is presented in Figure 6.2.

Joining instructions

Allow plenty of time to send out the joining instructions, say, at least 3–4 weeks before the course. These should give the participant sufficient detail as to the arrangements and organisation of the course. Any pre-course requirements must be included in the briefing pack, for example, read a paper, complete the questionnaire, bring it with you. For those delegates unfamiliar with the venue, it is always useful to include map and transportation details.

Figure 6.2   Sample application form

Title (e.g. Dr/Mr/Mrs):   Surname/family name: Forename:
Membership no.
Position/job title:
Organisation:
Address:
Post code/zip code: Country:
Tel.:   Mobile:
Fax: E-mail:

Please reserve a place for me on the following course/activity
Course title:
Course date:
Course location:

Method of payment
Course fee (amount and currency, e.g. dollar, pound, euro):
(a) Please invoice my organisation:
Contact details (if different from above):
(b) Cheque enclosed for ....
(Please make cheque payable to ....)
(c) Credit or debit card (type, e.g. Visa, Mastercard, American Express):
Card holder name: Card number:
Start date: Expiry date:
Card holder signature:
(d) International money order

Cancellation fee details (e.g. non-returnable if cancelled less than two weeks before course)

Special needs (e.g. dietary, disabled access, hearing loop):

Please return this form to: (contact name and full contact details)

It may be worth reinforcing the need to be told of any special needs, for example, dietary, religious, wheelchair access.

Dress code now appears on many joining instructions, indicating the type of clothing to wear, for example, work clothes, casual attire or dress for comfort. For instance, some management courses run outdoor activities and therefore require appropriate clothing. Another course may require delegates to don safety equipment when entering underground stacks. Where participants are travelling from other countries it is useful to know the predicted temperature, weather forecast and suggested apparel.

The minimum details required in the joining instructions are:

- course name;
- level, e.g. introductory, advanced;
- course objective or learning outcomes;
- programme or agenda;
- any pre-course requirements, e.g. please read attached paper;
- date;
- time, e.g. 09.30–16.30;
- place, e.g. venue name and address, telephone number;
- map (attached or web address);
- transportation, e.g. public services, parking;
- any restrictions;
- catering – indicate if (and when) meals provided;
- course leader's details, e.g. trainer(s) and position or job title, and contact telephone number or e-mail address;
- other requirements, e.g. dietary or special needs;
- other details, e.g. please report to reception on arrival;
- contact name for any other queries.

Sample joining instructions are presented in Figure 6.3.

Venue

When planning a course, it is essential to book a suitable venue at the earliest opportunity. This may be anything from a meeting room to a hotel conference centre or commercial

Figure 6.3 Sample joining instructions

Organisation name
Address
Tel., Fax
E-mail
Web URL

Reference HCAApp001

Date

Dear

Course Name – Joining Instructions

Thank you for your application to attend the .... training course. The details are as follows:

- Title: How to critically appraised a scientific paper
- Level: introductory
- Date: 28 October
- Place: venue name and address, tel. number (map attached)
- Time: 09.30–16.30
- Catering: refreshments served from 09.15
- Buffet lunch provided
- Course leader or trainer and position or job title
- Contact number or e-mail details
- Course objectives and a programme are attached
- Pre-course requirements: please read attached paper
- Dress code: please dress for comfort
- Transportation: access by railway and number 16 bus
- Car parking must be reserved in advance

On arrival, please report to reception where staff will direct you to the training room. Please let me know if you are unable to attend so that your place may be offered to another candidate. If you have any dietary requirements, special needs or require further information, please contact me on [full contact details].

Yours sincerely

Course Organiser

site. The venue must be able to cope with all your requirements – from equipment or Internet access to air conditioning, as well as covering health and safety. Other considerations will be the cost to hire or use the venue, catering, hire of equipment, delegate rates. Attention should be paid to issues such as noise, convenience to public transport, and disabled facilities.

Venue checklist

Check off the following when planning a course:

- assess venue costs;
- book date(s) and confirm;
- access restrictions
  - access to building or room – before, during and after the course;
  - security passes, keys;
- catering
  - dietary, religious and special needs
  - for how many? at what times?
- equipment
  - availability, cost;
  - allowed to use own equipment – does it need a safety check?
  - access to technician;
  - stationery, e.g. pins, tape;
- room(s)
  - number required, e.g. plenary and breakout (or syndicate) rooms;
  - distance between rooms;
  - suitability
    - size, shape, acoustics, blinds, windows, ventilation, temperature;
    - furniture, e.g. tables, chairs;

Figure 6.4 Room layouts

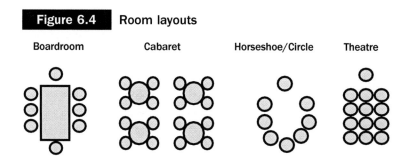

- style – boardroom, cabaret, horseshoe, theatre (see Figure 6.4);
- plug sockets – numbers, locations;
- external influences, e.g. noise, fire alarm tests, window cleaning;
- health and safety, e.g. fire escapes, evacuation procedures;
- facilities, e.g. toilets, lifts, ramps;
- registration/reception/signage;
- transportation, e.g. public transport, car parks, taxi services.

Presenters/trainers/speaker

A number of factors should be considered when selecting the trainer or presenter. It is worth looking at the individual's credentials. Not only must the person be an authority on the subject area, but they must also possess excellent presentation skills and be capable of putting across facts and information in an interesting and informative way. The presenter needs to engender rapport with the audience and be in control of the session, for example, handling conflict, helping participants, and varying the pace. Other aspects to consider when arranging a speaker will be their availability and fees. Ensure that this person is good value for money and check if there are any contractual obligations. Some organisations require external speakers to be registered or vetted. Agreement must be reached as regards what the speaker's fees will cover, for example, preparation, travelling expenses, courseware and the method of payment.

Before the commencement of a course, the trainer should be provided with the list of participants and note if there are any special requirements. The trainer's brief needs to reinforce such things as professional conduct and emphasise the need to meet the learning objectives. Course organisers should check on what equipment the trainer will need and whether there are any presentations to be loaded or handouts to be copied.

Development of courseware

A number of options are available to anyone involved in courseware development. These range from buying an off-the-shelf package, adapting another person's ideas, to customising existing material or writing and designing your own. Some material may require licensing or permission to use, while other material might have restrictions or limitations. All have implications for copyright, and any adapted or amended material must acknowledge the originator.

However the courseware is developed, it must be relevant and appropriate to the intended audience. Write in language familiar to the audience, clarifying any abbreviations or acronyms, and limit the use of technical terms unless they are the jargon of the speciality. Know in what formats you will require your material to be presented, for example, workbooks, presentation package, handouts and/or audiovisual aids. If using a presentation package to print off handouts, decide how many slides there will be to a page. Never use more than six to a page. A number of trainers produce their delegate handouts by selecting or adapting slides from the main presentation, i.e. one set of slides for the presentation and a separate set for the audience.

The norms applied to the design, writing and development of courseware are:

- one hour of preparation equals one minute of presentation;
- KISS-KIL – keep it simple and short, keep it lean;
- deliver what can be absorbed;
- audiovisual aids must add value, not detract from the message.

Running the course

Good practice means that the trainer will arrive well in advance of the session. This is to ensure that all arrangements are satisfactory and checks have been made of equipment and facilities. Be prepared to troubleshoot; for instance, a situation may arise that requires drastic changes to the programme, such as power failure, no Internet connection, room double booked. Think about what you will do if half the course delegates do not turn up, arrive late or numbers exceed expectations.

Set up the room(s) how you want it (them) arranged. The main plenary session may be in a horseshoe, while breakout rooms have tables and chairs. Ensure that all equipment is working and you know how to operate the controls.

Checklist:

- rooms
  - chairs, tables;

- style, e.g. boardroom, cabaret, horseshoe (circle) or theatre;
- proximity to each other;
- equipment
  - know how it works;
  - adequate for needs;
  - stationery, e.g. paper, pens;
- material
  - courseware, e.g. handouts, workbooks, presentation;
  - paper, pens;
- catering
  - refreshments;
  - meals;
- domestic amenities
  - toilets;
  - environment, e.g. air conditioning, heating;
- health and safety, e.g. cables, fire exits, emergency procedures;
- signposted;
- reception made aware of session;
- troubleshooting, e.g. adapt or make alterations.

There are many excellent books on public speaking and presentation skills. As such, this chapter does not examine the subject in depth, and instead is limited to the following useful pointers. Greet the participants and make them feel welcome. Most courses begin with domestic notices. Give a clear remit about the course and explain what the programme will/will not cover. Create an atmosphere conducive to learning. It is important to keep to time, particularly around comfort or refreshment breaks, but build in flexibility. Know where and when you will take questions.

Talk to the audience not the screen or audiovisual equipment. Where presentation packages are used, caution should be exercised to avoid:

- using too many slides – they should only be used as an aide memoir;

- reading from the slides, thereby turning your back on the audience; and

- sending the audience to sleep through sheer boredom.

Check back with participants before proceeding to the next session or activity. Use methods appropriate to the session and never lose the message that you are trying to convey. Be prepared to curtail the session if the audience is bored, asleep or showing signs of overload.

Training methods

Training and development activities may be undertaken using a range of methods and techniques. A selection of the more popular techniques is given below. The reader may recognise the explanations but use different terminology. There are numerous variations on the following ideas. Some techniques are more suited to courses or large group activities.

- Analogy:
  - Teaching strategy that makes the unfamiliar familiar.
  - Defined as a likeness or similarity between two things that are otherwise unalike.

- Enhances understanding of complex concepts or abstractions by allowing learners to consider the concepts in a different context.
- Strategy may be used in a variety of settings (classroom, library) and may be used with large or small groups, or as an individual assignment.

■ Action learning/action learning set:

- Current or live issues are used to confront and solve problems that draw on the experience and expertise of group members.
- Questioning concepts and ideas is encouraged.
- The group is self-managed and self-directed.

■ Ad hoc/base method:

- A series of bases is set up on various topics; delegates visit each base in turn. Bases are often skills related, short training sessions, hands-on practical activities.

■ Brainstorming:

- Note down as many words or thoughts as possible – random, spontaneous, no ranking, no order, no priority.
- Works by stimulating thought, often bouncing ideas off someone else.
- Uses an element of energy.
- Often a fun activity.
- Outcomes can be used to help formulate a session, project or other result by examining each suggestion then accepting or rejecting for a sound reason.

■ Buzz groups:

- Between two or three people in a group discussing ideas and thoughts.
- May use similar techniques to brainstorming.

- Case studies:
  - A series of facts relating to a particular situation is given in which the individual or group has to ask a series of questions or come to an agreement in order to present a solution.
  - Involves an analysis of a situation or incident that depicts an actual or fictitious scenario.
  - Can range from very simple to complex.
  - Presents information to the group to be followed by questions.
  - Allows students to learn concepts and diagnostic reasoning in a specific context.
  - Critical thinking occurs when questions involve problem solving as opposed to interpretation of facts.
- Concept map:
  - Used to show and facilitate understanding of conceptual relationships.
  - Facilitate communication between students and faculty.
  - Students draw maps showing problems and how these problems are interrelated – result may resemble a mind map or neural network.
- Debate:
  - Involves the construction of argument to defend a position.
  - Excellent strategy for teaching critical thinking because it requires reasoning skills, analysis of multiple relationships, and consideration of multiple perspectives.
  - Teaching strategy is best applied to topics involving controversy or dilemma, particularly ethical or legal problems.

- Demonstration:
  - A means of showing participants how a task or skill should be executed.
  - Participants should be afforded the time to practise.
- Discovery learning:
  - Combination of brainstorming, buzz groups, role play and other methods in which a group of people explore a topic by exchanging views and experiences and having a go.
- Exercises:
  - A process in which an individual or group is asked to undertake a specific task leading to a specific result.
  - Often part of a practical skills improvement, may test learning or understanding.
- Games:
  - Only eight games, all others are variations on:
    - energetic or group games (good spirited; sometimes individual success);
    - relays (disciplined, competitive);
    - team or cooperation (sportsmanship, often competitive);
    - skills (empirical, experimental);
    - sense training (mind, observation);
    - in-tray or management (quiet, relaxation. perception, using faculties);
    - acting or role play (imaginative, confidence-building);
    - wide games – (played across a wide area, exploration, outdoors), e.g. raid (stealth); cordon break; treasure hunt; man hunt (hunter-killer).

- Not all games have winners and losers.
- Learning by doing. Building on experience. Must have clearly defined rules.
- See also quizzes and puzzles, below.

- Goldfish bowl:
  - Presentation of a problems or set of facts, group explores ways of finding solution then elects a representative.
  - Representatives from each group meet to form a core group in the centre of the room.
  - Purpose is to present case for own group and explore solutions with other representatives.
  - Remainder of course sit behind representative – they may not talk during the core discussion, only observe body language and listen to conversation.
  - Roles may be assigned to representatives before central discussion, e.g. do not put forward your group's views; be argumentative.
  - Feedback from groups – how well was group represented? Were views put across? What outcomes from the discussion? Other observations?

- Group work:
  - Small number of people brought together for an activity or series of events.
  - Groups may be random or carefully structured for a given situation.
  - Discussion and debate; builds on experience and expertise; challenging.
  - Work together to produce a result or outcome.
  - Likely to involve other training methods in process and test leadership skills.

- Jigsaw:
  - Cooperative learning strategy that involves group learning.
  - Each group is given a task or problem within a package of information.
  - Each group member is given a 'piece of a puzzle' to learn.
  - Each member then shares what they have learned with other group members.
  - Goal is that all group members eventually learn by bringing all the pieces of the jigsaw together to solve the problem
  - If there are a number of groups then each group can be given a piece of puzzle to solve, to then bring together with the other groups.
  - Depends on each individual in order to accomplish the task.
- Icebreakers or energisers (see Appendix D for a selection of icebreakers):
  - Used at the beginning of the course to stimulate and energise the participants.
  - Useful way to get people talking or interacting.
- Lectures, seminars, conferences:
  - Where one or more persons convey information to participants by talking; may include audiovisual material or other aids.
  - Formal, usually in classroom-based mode.
  - Subject matter defined in advance of delivery date.
  - Occasionally may be participative, more likely to be listening with options to ask questions.
  - Usually has feedback or evaluation at end of process.

- Mind Maps (Mind Maps originated in 1970 by Tony Buzan; Mind Map is a registered trademark of the Buzan Organisation).

  - Builds up a web or map of ideas and associated topics.

  - All terms interrelated with hooks to other terms.

  - No sequencing or order, capturing thoughts as quickly as possible.

  - Can cluster or colour code results to focus the eye and brain.

  - Adds to imagery.

- One-to-one:

  - Mentoring and coaching individual to identify problems and find solutions.

  - Requires questioning techniques, listening and observation skills.

  - Ability to stimulate thought.

  - Draws on experience.

- PEST analysis:

  - Uses a matrix to identify areas that may affect or influence a problem or issue.

  - Matrix used to analyse situation against four areas:

    - political – laws, regulations, codes, pressure groups;

    - economic – finance, costs, markets, demands, labour;

    - social – living standards, norms, education, care, health;

    - technical – equipment, machinery, systems, processes, inventions.

- Plenary:
  - Whole course or delegation brought together for one purpose, e.g. tuition, open forum, receiving instructions from session leader.
  - Often used to introduce a session during a course before completing an exercise or activity.
- Problem-based learning:
  - Involves group problem-solving with real-life situations (case or scenario) to stimulate critical thinking.
  - Process of discovery – students learn by working through an activity; content is self-taught by the group.
  - Brief is presented to the group describing the situation but not the problem.
  - Learners within a group must identify key issues and determine what additional information is needed.
  - Through the process of discussion and discovery, the group arrives at solutions to the problem.
- Project work:
  - Groups brought together to fulfil a specific task.
  - May be real-life scenario, i.e. not part of a course.
  - Uses project management techniques.
  - Requires aims, objectives, methods, implementation, evaluation.
  - Time-bound.
  - Microcosm of the macrocosm.
- Quizzes and puzzles:
  - Means of introducing a subject in an often humorous way.
  - Tests general and specific knowledge.

- Yes-no, sets, options, multi-choice.
- Bingo, board games, tangram, enigmas, crosswords or number play.

■ Role play:

- Dramatisation of an event or situation – usually represents a problem or difference between individuals, or a conflict situation.
- Act out a scene or scenario with good and bad practices.
- Unscripted scenario with the learners acting out a problem in a spontaneous manner.
- Useful strategy for practising therapeutic communication skills and dealing with conflict.
- Can be used for small-scale ideas of large productions.
- Evaluation of impact, presentation.
- Some people feel very uncomfortable with false situation, or feel mocked.
- Opportunity to use well-briefed professional actors.

■ Round table:

- Combines elements of buzz group and brainstorming. Each person has to think of an idea or contribute one item to the discussion.
- Usually work systematically round the table or group.
- Individual may be asked to justify reasons (brainstorming with complexity).

■ Self-taught/self-directed learning:

- Individuals are afforded the opportunity to learn, enhance or develop their own skills or abilities.
- Tests initiative and understanding, may require assistance.

- May be part of distance learning or e-learning activity.
- Simulation:
  - Involves controlled representations of events (usually in a laboratory setting).
  - Strategy allows the learner to experience 'real-world' situations without risk.
  - Learners are required to assess and interpret the situation, and make decisions based on information provided.
  - Allows students to practise a variety of skills, assess situations and make decisions.
- Skills training:
  - Training for a specific skill, sometimes on a one-to-one basis with an expert.
  - Imparting knowledge to a novice.
  - Almost always of a practical nature.
- SWOT or SW(O)OT:
  - Adds structure to brainstorming.
  - Matrix:
    - strengths and weakness – current and internal;
    - opportunities and threats – future and external;
    - obstacles.
  - Work on outcomes:
    - turning weakness into strengths;
    - turning threats into opportunities;
    - overcoming obstacles.
  - Sometimes used in personal analysis.
- Video taping:
  - Recording an activity or presentation then playing back to the individual, group or class.

- Useful way in which the individual can see and evaluate their own performance.
- Requires constructive feedback – highlighting good points, and suggesting improvements to areas of poor delivery.
- Many people feel uncomfortable or threatened by this method.

■ Worksheets:

- Material brought together for individuals and groups to work through.
- May take the form of a checklist, matrix, tick-box, yes-no answer sheet.
- Sometimes uses short scenarios as a starting point for discussion.
- May be used to test understanding about a topic or procedure.
- Analysis often done on results or outcomes, particularly from group activities.
- Results may be retained by individual if they are of a personal nature.

Equipment and materials

The equipment used should be relevant or appropriate to the training session. The trainer needs to know how the equipment works and what to do if it goes wrong or breaks down. An overhead projector and one acetate slide may be more effective than 20 PowerPoint slides. The audience will get frustrated if the trainer is constantly switching between equipment, such as projector, video, DVD and laptop.

Some pointers on using the equipment:

- Make a checklist of all the equipment you will need.

- Check all equipment before the start of the course.

- Have equipment set up ready for use.

- Know how to use the equipment.

- Check power sources in room, e.g. extension leads, adapters.

- Have everything in the correct order, e.g. equipment, handouts.

- Have materials labelled or packaged ready for action.

- Do not rummage, fiddle or fumble.

- Take time to get the equipment the way you want it before proceeding.

- Synchronise the equipment with the presentation.

- Talk to the audience not the screen, desk or other fitments.

- Make contingency plans.

- Make back-ups of material (if need be in other formats).

- Take everything in your stride – don't get flustered.

- Check on insurance – what is covered under policy.

- Check on licenses, copyright, legal requirements.

- Audio systems:

  - which way to load a cassette;

  - how to play a CD or tape;

  - controls to pause, fast forward, rewind and adjust volume;

  - speakers, amplifier.

- Computers:
  - familiarity with system;
  - back-up;
  - check plug sockets in room;
  - know how to use the mouse, keys and other facilities;
  - know how to attach peripheral components, e.g. printers;
  - copying, saving and deleting;
  - drives (A, C, D, E);
  - disks, CDs, DVDs, memory sticks.
- Courseware material including handouts/workbooks:
  - sufficient numbers;
  - correct order;
  - labelled or packaged;
  - licensed;
  - add value;
  - relevant;
  - space for notes;
  - referring to other sources;
  - attractive.
- Display boards:
  - know how to erect;
  - design of display – symmetry, asymmetry, radial;
  - mounting material – drawing pins, Velcro, adhesive tack, magnets.
- Flipcharts:
  - know how to put up a flipchart easel;
  - sufficient paper;

- write in upper or lower case – legible size;
- pens, e.g. use black, brown, blue, purple; do not use red, green, yellow, orange;
- use feint lines to assist with presentations.
- LCD projectors:
  - know how to connect into other equipment;
  - focus and other facilities, e.g. zoom;
  - toggle the screens;
  - volume control;
  - remote controls (and batteries).
- Overhead projector (OHP):
  - know how to dismantle and clean;
  - know how to change the bulb;
  - check the focus (get rid of the blue or yellow haze);
  - decide whether to turn on and off between slides;
  - position slide before starting to talk.
- Screen:
  - how to put up or secure a screen;
  - no screen – what other options to use, e.g. wall, whiteboard, flipchart paper.
- Slide projector:
  - carousel;
  - which way up the slides go;
  - slides in correct order;
  - black-out slide;
  - removing stuck slide;
  - using the remote control;
  - focus.

- Smart boards:
  - wired into to computer system;
  - smart pens;
  - know how to use the software;
  - convert, save, delete material.
- Son-et-lumière:
  - synchronisation of equipment, e.g. sound and vision;
  - may use slide projector and tape recorder.
- Telephone lines:
  - line in room;
  - facilities to link into the telephone systems;
  - able to get an outside line;
  - know the telephone number;
  - broadband/dial-up.
- Television and video/DVD:
  - controls;
  - correct channel;
  - fast forward and rewind;
  - pause;
  - volume;
  - remote controls (and batteries).
- Three-dimensional displays.
  - facility to display;
  - protection against breakage;
  - suitable surfaces.
- Transparencies.
  - clear, concise;

- aide-memoir;
- font, point size.
- Video camera/camcorder:
  - how to use, e.g. handling, focus, tripod, positioning;
  - correct way to load video cassette;
  - playback facilities;
  - interacting with other equipment.
- Whiteboards:
  - correct pens;
  - cleaning solutions;
  - pen colours – black, blue, brown, purple.

7

Selected course examples

This chapter lists some examples of courses or workshops that have been run for staff working in the library and information profession. They have been selected to show the diverse range of training that needs to be undertaken by staff if they are to stay fit for purpose in the workplace. The examples given indicate the learning outcome that one would expect to achieve at the end of the course. Most of the courses are progressive in that they can be run at different levels, i.e. basic or introductory, intermediate, and advanced or specialised. Much depends on the role of the individual as to the depth of complexity of knowledge required from a course. Not all staff would need to progress to the highest level.

AACR2: intermediate

AACR2 (Anglo American Cataloguing Rules 2nd edition revised) is the acknowledged standard for cataloguing material. Librarians need to have a working knowledge of the rules, as this will help them understand the requirements of the MARC 21 format that they underpin.

By the end of the course, participants will know how to:

- Navigate AACR2 securely to find information.
- Describe a range of media using the format.
- Construct headings that comply with AACR2.

- Build AACR2 descriptors.
- Establish consistent forms of name for individuals and organisations.
- Understand the relationship between AACR2 and MARC 21.
- Use AACR2 effectively to improve MARC21 work.

Abstracting: intermediate

Abstracting and précis techniques are essential for scanning documents, compiling current awareness services, preparing briefings, summarising reports, answering enquiries and undertaking desk research.

By the end of the course, participants will know how to:

- Develop strategies for summarising the content of different material.
- Scan documents quickly to identify their key content.
- Identify and use different abstract formats.
- Extract and summarise the main information
  - What should be included or omitted.
- Write and present the abstracted details using different word lengths.
- Describe a book's content.
- Summarise journal articles.
- Write and abstract a technical report.

Assertiveness: introduction

Staff must be able to communicate effectively with colleagues and users in a firm and positive way. This means staying in control of emotions and being able to handle difficult situations.

By the end of the course, participants will know how to:

- Recognise the different forms of assertive behaviour
  - Implement assertiveness techniques including saying 'no'.
- Defuse difficult situations and resolve conflict in the workplace.
- Deal confidently with difficult users and reach a positive solution.
- Manage user expectations and respond to awkward user behaviour.
- Use effective questioning and listening skills.
- Interpret non-verbal communications.

Business planning: introduction

All aspects of society require business plans to be drawn up. These define the main functions of the organisation and indicate future development as short-term, medium-term and long-term plans.

By the end of the course, participants will know how to:

- Define the purpose of developing strategic business plans.
- Examine the requirements for the development of effective plans.
- Evaluate the need for short and long-term objectives.
- Produce a draft outline for a strategic business plan.
- Create Gantt charts.

Cataloguing and classification: introduction

The organisation of knowledge is central to the effective function of any library and information service. It is crucial that librarians understand how to apply the principles of cataloguing and classification.

By the end of the course, participants will know how to:

- Apply AACR2.
- Interpret the main international standards for classifying documents
  - Dewey Decimal Classification;
  - UDC.
- Apply subject headings.
- Tailor the standards for in-house usage including computer format.
- Use descriptive cataloguing, classification and subject description.
- Select the classification scheme for specialist collections (e.g. medicine, law).

Communication skills: introduction

Communication looks easy when it is done well, but there is convincing evidence that it is poorly applied in the workplace. Maintaining effective communication with staff, colleagues and users underpins all functions of library and information services.

By the end of the course, participants will know how to:

- Define the main principles of communications both verbal and non-verbal.

- Apply good listening, observation and questioning skills.
- Liaise with colleagues, staff and users.
- Communicate in a variety of formats, media and styles e.g.
  - written, oral;
  - telephone, e-mail, face-to-face;
  - writing and giving instructions.

Copyright and intellectual property: introduction

Librarians must be aware of the implications of copyright and regulations related to intellectual property, and how they affect the work undertaken in library and information services. This includes licensing, limitations on use and charging.

By the end of the course, participants will know how to:

- Interpret the legal requirement of the statutes covering copyright
  - limitation and exceptions;
  - different formats and media, e.g. music, books, electronic.
- Evaluate the role of copyright in the workplace.
- Make distinctions between copying for a commercial or a non-commercial purpose.
- Apply for licenses to cover work activities.
- Produce current awareness services by staying within the law.
- Seek further guidance from licensing agencies.

Copyright in the electronic age: intermediate

Increased digitisation means that electronic copyright often needs to be treated differently to other formats to retain its protection under law. This includes websites, broadcasts, databases, photographic images, scanning of hard copy material and a number of other formats. Staff need to have a good understanding of the problems caused by new technology and how legislation addresses these issues.

By the end of the course, participants will know how to:

- Apply the legal requirements (statutes and case law) under the copyright laws
  - digital rights management;
  - licences.
- Interpret the law with regard to websites, broadcasts, databases, scanning material from hard copy, photographic and pictorial images, digital signatures.
- Obtain copyright clearance of digital content.

Core library and information skills: introduction

Understanding how a library functions is a basic requirement for all staff working in an information setting. The core skills needed include keeping order, handling enquiries, retrieving information and being aware of the main sources and resources.

By the end of the course, participants will know how to:

- Handle enquiries by using questioning skills to ascertain requirements.

- Structure a simple search strategy to answer enquiries.

- Find and retrieve information from a variety of sources and resources including books, journals, Internet and databases.

- Use cataloguing and classification schemes, thesauri and other indices.

- Maintain order for the effective retrieval of information (e.g. shelving, filing).

- Promote the library service.

- Implement the policies and procedures required for library management.

Critical appraisal: intermediate

Being able to critically appraise a technical report, scientific articles or a website is increasingly becoming part of the librarian's remit. This requires the techniques to assess and validate information for its credibility and robustness.

By the end of the course, participants will know how to:

- Define the techniques and methods used in critical appraisal.

- Critically appraise a research article.

- Review electronic resources such as web pages for authenticity, credibility and validity.

- Examine the requirements to produce a critical appraisal digest.

- Analyse the librarian's role in critically appraising resources.

Customer services: introduction

Customer service is fundamental to the work of library and information services. Being able to establish a rapport with users to discuss and respond to their needs is crucial in the workplace.

By the end of the course, participants will know how to:

- Understand and predict customer needs.

- Discuss ways of providing the customer with the most appropriate material and information.

- Build rapport and communicate effectively with customers using a variety of ways

  - body language, voice tone and words;

  - face-to-face, written, telephone, e-mail.

- Handle difficult customers and situations.

- Communicate effectively with different user types.

- Measure customer satisfaction using different tools, e.g. compiling questionnaires.

- Write an action plan to create a more customer-focused environment.

Customer services – dealing with difficult users: intermediate

Increasingly, LIS staff have to deal with difficult and potentially aggressive users. Being able to manage and defuse conflict situations is integral to producing a satisfactory outcome in customer relations.

By the end of the course, participants will know how to:

- Develop policies and strategies for handling difficult situations.

- Assess the potential and real risks of dealing with conflict situations within libraries.

- Develop appropriate responses to a range of incidents.

- Reduce levels of stress and anxiety in the workplace.

- Put preventative measures in place to reduce future conflict scenarios.

Data protection and freedom of information: introduction

Many libraries are required to balance the needs for openness and transparency of information against the protection of personal data. This is not about censorship but compliance with legislation and preventing the misuse of information.

By the end of the course, participants will know how to:

- Define the main principles of data protection and freedom of information

  - exemptions, access, transfer, notification and subject rights.

- Implement the legal requirements to maintain manual and electronic systems relating to personal information.

- Differentiate between public information and personal data.

- Deal with requests for information under data protection or freedom of information.

- Handle transborder flow of information to countries without the equivalent legislative safeguards.

Designing a library database: introduction

Understanding the way to design a simple database can be a cost-effective alternative to buying and customising an off-the-shelf package.

By the end of the course, participants will know how to:

- Write a simple database specification.
- Identify and use the main components, tools and features of a database.
- Create a textbase, add fields and other attributes.
- Add, amend and edit records.
- Create tables, reports, forms, queries and user interfaces.
- Customise toolbars and set user preferences.

Designing a library database: intermediate

Being able to develop and expand the functions of a housekeeping database can enhance the activities within library and information services. Understanding how to manipulate text easily and carefully can make better use of staff time and safeguard textbases.

By the end of the course, participants will know how to:

- Manipulate text.
- Structure tables and develop relationships.
- Apply database security and good housekeeping practices.
- Create a number of related database tables.
- Explore the different options when exporting or importing records.
- Copy, rename, delete, and back-up textbases.

Designing a library database: advanced

In many instances, information staff rather than the IT department maintain the library databases. This is because of their specialist nature. Whoever is responsible for the maintenance and upkeep of the databases needs an understanding of the more advanced techniques of design, development and usage.

By the end of the course, participants will know how to:

- Link textbases.

- Edit secondary textbases.

- Import material from other sources.

- Dump and reload textbases.

- Design forms, menus and batch modify.

Designing questionnaires and surveys: intermediate

Librarians need to use surveys and questionnaires to ensure that their services stay relevant and fit for purpose.

By the end of the course, participants will know how to:

- Formulate clear aims and objectives.

- Conduct questionnaires and survey using different methods
    - identify the advantages and disadvantages of each method.

- Prepare and conduct structured interviews.

- Capture and record data.

- Analyse, collate and interpret the results.

- qualitative;
- quantitative.

■ Write up the findings.

Desk research skills: introduction

Library and information staff often carry out detailed desk research and need to develop their research and retrieval skills.

By the end of the course, participants will know how to:

■ Conduct a reference interview to clarify the depth and level of information required.

■ Formulate a desk research strategy.

■ Carry out research using the most appropriate method.

■ Identify and evaluate sources of information.

■ Use search engines, indexes, abstracts and other tools to retrieve information.

■ Present the findings in the required format.

Developing a policy for the digital collection: advanced

In the digital age, librarians are expected to manage and develop traditional and virtual online collections of material. Irrespective of the media, collection management involves the selection, acquisition, storage, dissemination, evaluation, preservation and promotion of the material. All libraries should have a collection development policy that embodies traditional physical collections and embraces their digital resources.

By the end of the course, participants will know how to:

■ Identify the nature and content of a collection development policy.

- Promote the policy within the organisation and to users.

- Review the policy issues surrounding e-resources and how these differ from other resources.

- Evaluate the policy with reference to physical and digital collections.

E-mail and online communications: introduction

Using electronic means to communicate with colleagues is now the norm, but being able to do it effectively is equally important.

By the end of the course, participants will know how to:

- Set up and use an e-mail account – creating, sending, replying and forwarding e-mails.

- Manage and maintain an e-mail account – saving, filing, archiving, deleting.

- Activate web-based e-mail services and remote access.

- Sign up for and participate in e-mail discussion lists and chat rooms.

- Implement protective measure – virus protection, spyware, washers, spam filters.

Facilitation skills: introduction

Facilitation is the skill of being able to work with small and large groups in a training situation to maximise learning and development.

By the end of the course, participants will know how to:

- Work with small groups to enable a training activity to be carried out.

- Assess the ways in which people learn.

- Assess the needs of the group.

- Use a variety of methods to enhance the learning activity.

- Encourage and promote discussion.

- Handle group dynamics through all five stages – forming, storming, norming, performing, mourning.

- Use facilitation to aid decision-making and problem-solving.

Finance for the non-financial manager: introduction

Maintaining a service that stays fit for purpose means ensuring that library monies are spent on pertinent and relevant materials. Being able to handle finances and budgets against a background of constrained resources is a crucial operation of library and information services.

By the end of the course, participants will know how to:

- Produce a financial strategy in line with organisational requirements.

- Prepare and maintain ledgers, budgets and accounts.

- Create and use spreadsheets as part of good financial practice.

- Distinguish between capital and revenue finance transactions.

- Compare key financial performance indicators.

- Assess critical factors with respect to value for money activities and purchases.

Induction course: introduction

Induction courses give a valuable insight into the structure function and role of an organisation. This provides an opportunity to promote the library and information services to new staff and potential users. Induction courses are a useful way to meet colleagues.

By the end of the course participants will know about:

- Role and function of the parent organisation
  - structure, activities, culture.
- Role and function of library and information services
  - broad overview of services.

Instruction techniques: introduction

To train other people, staff must have good instructional skills, whether this is for one-to-one training or large group instruction.

By the end of the course, participants will know how to:

- Give training instructions to
  - different size groups;
  - different levels.
- Use a variety of techniques for different audiences or occasions.
- Write effective instructions.

Internet efficiency: introduction

Technology moves at a fast pace, so it is important that staff understand how the Internet works and what role it plays in the information world.

By the end of the course, participants will know how to:

- Explore the functions, services and structure of the Internet.
- Get the most from the browser, printing, bookmarks and the history function.
- Use the tools for navigation and retrieval purposes.
- Examine the type of information accessible through the Internet.
- Save and download data.

Interlibrary loans: introduction

To enable access to wider collections of material, most libraries engage in interlibrary loan activities using a document delivery service.

By the end of the course, participants will know how to:

- Review available resources to fulfil the user's requests for interlibrary loans.
- Request material from other participating information services.
- Handle procedures for dealing with requests in different formats, e.g. paper, fax, electronic.
- Comply with the rules and regulations relating to interlibrary loans and document delivery.
- Implement charging for interlibrary loans.
- Budget for interlibrary loan services.

Library of Congress Subject Headings: intermediate

The Library of Congress Subject Headings (LCSH) have become the de facto form of language-based subject access for libraries. The use of the MARC 21 authority format for LCSH has been shown to maintain coherence in the use of headings in a database.

By the end of the course, participants will know how to:

- Build simple and complex subject headings using LCSH in MARC 21 bibliographic format.

- Select basic headings and navigate the subheadings.

- Deal with matters geographical.

Management skills: introduction

Management applies to all personnel working in a library setting. The three mains areas are managing yourself, managing time, managing a resource and for some, the fourth is managing other people.

By the end of the course, participants will know how to:

- Analyse and assess personal strengths and weaknesses.

- Improve communications by recognising your own and others' behaviour.

- Promote improved performance through good management practice.

- Define group dynamics with a view to developing effective team members.

- Motivate staff and make the work environment conducive to work activity.

- Manage conflict situations.

- Recognise the skills needed for effective leadership.

- Approach decision-making and problem-solving dilemmas.

- Manage self, time and resources more effectively.

Management of change: introduction

'The only constant we know is change', and change is happening at a faster rate than any time in history. It can be a platform for hope, inspiration and modernisation or one for despair, resistance and demotivation.

By the end of the course, participants will know how to:

- Identify the features and stages of a change process.
- Interpret facts from fiction and realities from myths.
- Deal with the resistance and differing responses to change in the workplace.
- Communicate with staff during a period of change and uncertainty.
- Implement strategies to motivate staff.
- Minimise disruption to work activities during a change process.

Managing meetings: introduction

It is almost impossible to be in a work environment and not have to attend meetings. Good practices can make meetings highly relevant while bad practices make them a waste of time.

By the end of the course, participants will know how to:

- Plan and administer meetings effectively – before, during and after the meeting.
- Recognise the need for different meetings in the workplace.
- Communicate effectively during meetings.
- Chair and manage the dynamics of a meeting.
- Implement team meetings and team briefings.

- Carry out the function of each role – chairing, secretarial, minute taking.

Managing staff development and training: advanced

Senior LIS professionals must possess the knowledge and skills needed to plan, deliver and evaluate a staff training and development programme.

By the end of the course, participants will know how to:

- Appraise staff to ascertain training and development needs.

- Create a training and development plan.

- Set learning and training objectives for themselves and their staff.

- Evaluate training and development events, activities and the programme.

- Promote training events.

- Recruit external agencies to deliver training activities.

MARC 21: intermediate

MARC 21 is the only quality metadata format currently available and provides a model for how this area of work should be approached. Sound knowledge of MARC 21 is a key element when cataloguing in an online environment. MARC 21 may be applied to a range of formats (books, serials, videos and electronic resources).

By the end of the course, participants will know how to:

- Apply an integrated approach to the MARC 21 format.

- Use the basic elements of the MARC bibliographic format.

- Fill out the format for different fields

  - notes fields (500), fixed field 008;

  - name headings and uniform titles.

- Assess the impact of the Library of Congress and the Programme for Cooperative Cataloguing on the quality of MARC 21.

- Relate MARC 21 authority format with AACR.

Marketing library and information services: introduction

At some time libraries will need to promote and market their services to a number of different users.

By the end of the course, participants will know how to:

- Write a marketing plan to promote the library and information service

  - set clear marketing objectives as part of a winning strategy.

- Implement a marketing strategy in the workplace.

- Produce a set of tools and techniques to use in marketing planning.

- Create attention-grabbing marketing communications techniques.

Marketing promotional literature: intermediate

It is not enough to have a marketing strategy without thinking about the type of literature needed to promote the service. Such things as newsletters, pamphlets and posters all play a key role in raising the profile of the service.

By the end of the course, participants will know how to:

- Use a range of techniques to produce promotional material to advertise their services.

- Design brochures, leaflets, posters and other promotional literature.

- Promote events and themed activities.

- Develop the groundwork for a publicity campaign to promote a library event.

- Use visual impact to maximum benefit – style, format, aesthetics, illustrations, novelty.

- Display and exhibit promotional literature – from noticeboards to conferences.

Online tools – RSS, blogs and wikis: introduction

Being able to keep up with the latest technological ideas, tools and developments is important when gathering, storing and disseminating information. Knowing how to use them effectively can enhance many activities within library and information services, from managing projects to current awareness and producing newsletters.

By the end of the course, participants will know how to:

- Define the role of RSS, blogs and wikis in an LIS context.

- Use RSS for current awareness and news alerts.

- Set up a blog.

- Identify relevant RSS feeds and blogs.

- Use RSS and blogs to market services and keep users up to date.

- Use blogs and wikis as collaborative tools.

Personal development: introduction

A personal development plan creates a clear plan of action for an individual to complete over a given period of time. The plan will cover areas of learning, objectives or goal setting, as well as defining gaps in development.

By the end of the course, participants will know how to:

- Define the elements of a personal development plan.
- Record achievements and progress, and measure against objectives.
- Use reflective practice to identify successes and difficulties.
- Evaluate their own training needs by identifying gaps in their learning.
- Write a personal development plan.

Presentation skills: introduction

Being able to stand in front of an audience and give a presentation can be a nerve-racking experience. It is possible to overcome such a fear with forward planning, knowing the right techniques to use and plenty of practice.

By the end of the course, participants will know how to:

- Plan a presentation.
- Identify the needs of the audience.
- Convey a message in a meaningful and effective way.
- Pitch the presentation at the correct level for the audience.
- Use different techniques to enhance a presentation.
- Use audiovisual equipment to create an impact.

Presentation skills package: introduction

Presentation skills packages are often used to during a talk or presentation. Effective use will enhance the talk, while poor use loses the message.

By the end of the course, participants will know how to:

- Create a simple slide presentation.
- Use different features such as fonts, colours and layouts to enhance the slides.
- Use graphics features to add value to a presentation.
- Print slides, notes and handouts.

Producing newsletters: introduction

An attractive and well-structured newsletter is a useful way of keeping staff informed of developments. As a communication tool they may cover a broad range of interests or be subject specific. They can be used to share ideas, market services or raise awareness of organisational issues.

By the end of the course, participants will know how to:

- Define the role of the newsletter for a variety of purposes.
- Research and analyse the target audience and its requirements.
- Design a successful newsletter (image, content, features, aesthetics, style, format).
- Write in a style that is appealing to the audience.
- Use desktop publishing to prepare and edit a newsletter.
- Circulate a newsletter using different media and formats.

Records management: introduction

Records management is increasingly becoming part of the remit of library and information services. It is particularly relevant where the library maintains organisational records for such things as company reports, correspondence files, legal and regulatory documents.

By the end of the course, participants will know how to:

- Write a records management strategy
  - lifecycle of a document;
  - retention scheduling;
  - disaster recovery plan.
- Design appropriate business classification scheme and file plans.
- Organise and file the records, manual and electronic, against defined criteria.
- Comply with the legal requirements for the storage and maintenance of company documents.
- Enforce the legislative and regulatory requirements such as freedom of information and data protection.

Reflective practice: introduction

A number of professional and vocational qualifications require librarians to reflect upon their experiences and expertise. Reflective practice involves a number of skills from the thought process through to analysis.

By the end of the course, participants will know how to:

- Reflect on their experiences, learning and growth (personal and professional).
- Use techniques and tools to evaluate and analyse performance.

- Write an analytical account of their personal performance.

- Structure a report that evaluates service performance against organisational objectives.

- Devise a forward-looking career plan.

- Assess future training and development needs.

Research skills: intermediate

Information professionals are increasingly required to undertake research and be able to present the results of their findings. Staff need to know and be able to use the main methodologies involved in research activities.

By the end of the course, participants will know how to:

- Define and structure a research question.

- Identify the different methodologies used in research.

- Create questionnaires or surveys to support the research.

- Locate evidence to support or refute the research question and recognise bias in the literature.

- Interpret and present the results of statistical analysis using qualitative and quantitative techniques.

- Write up the findings in a research report.

Strategic planning: advanced

Strategic planning is on a higher plain than business planning. It is easy to think in terms of operational task and short-term activities, to concentrate on this year rather than lay down long-term strategic plans.

By the end of the course, participants will know how to:

- Make informed decisions about the strategic direction of your service.

- Create a vision of your strategy – where you want your service to be in the short, medium and long term.

- Create a mission that encapsulates your vision.

- Lay the foundations for your strategy
  - overcoming barriers and threats;
  - creating opportunities.

- Write a strategic plan for the library and information service.

- Execute your strategy in a result-driven and purposeful way.

Searching skills: introduction

Searching for and retrieving information from a database are fundamental to the role of the library and information professional. All staff should be able to construct a simple search strategy to locate information in response to an enquiry.

By the end of the course, participants will know how to:

- Question users about their requirements.

- Construct a search strategy.

- Use terminology appropriate to the subject matter.

- Use simple Boolean logic and operators.

- Retrieve information from a database.

- Use features in the database or search engine to broaden or narrow the search.

- Refer complex enquiries to another person or authority.

Searching skills using the Internet: intermediate

Efficient searching of the Internet can be invaluable when dealing with enquiries. It is not enough to know how to create a search strategy or use a search engine; the art is in being able to use the tools effectively to retrieve the desired information from the millions of references.

By the end of the course, participants will know how to:

- Structure a search strategy using a variety of tools and operators.
- Refine search strategies to expand or reduce the number of hits retrieved.
- Use different search engines and know their limitations.
- Identify and bookmark authoritative sites for future reference.
- Navigate the World Wide Web to locate specific data.

Searching for evidence on the Internet: advanced

There is a wealth of information on the Internet, but being able to authenticate credible sources requires specialist information skills. These are sometimes referred to evidence-based assessments.

By the end of the course, participants will know how to:

- Identify and evaluate credible sources of information on the Internet.
- Use search engines and subject directories to find evidence-based material.
- Construct effective Internet searches.

- Critically appraise and systematically review the sources of information.

- Consider the advantages and disadvantages of using the Internet for specialist information enquiries.

- Use discussion lists, URLs and other tools to find evidence.

Service level agreements: introduction

It is sometimes necessary to enter into a contractual arrangement or service level agreement with another agent or third party. Service level agreements define the terms and conditions under which a service will be provided.

By the end of the course, participants will know how to:

- Identify the role and function of service level agreements.

- Summarise the main points when negotiating a service level agreement.

- Outline the main elements for inclusion in a service level agreement.

- Draft a model service level agreement template.

Spreadsheets: introduction

Spreadsheets are widely used in library and information services to record data, or maintain housekeeping records or financial accounts.

By the end of the course, participants will know how to:

- Create and save a simple spreadsheet.

- Use embellishments to enhance the document.

- Manipulate data using cut, copy and paste facilities.

- Create simple formulae to add up columns and use totals.

Supervisory skills: introduction

Although a person may not manage staff, they often have a supervisory role either in the training or overseeing a work activity.

By the end of the course, participants will know how to:

- Define their role as a supervisor and manage their own workload.

- Define the factors that motivate staff to perform well – job satisfaction and dissatisfaction.

- Provide instruction to staff on a given technique or activity.

- Allocate or delegate work and set goals.

- Brief staff and keep them informed.

- Give and receive praise, criticism and feedback.

Thesaurus construction: introduction

The need for intelligent control of subject access to increasingly complex data is becoming more evident. Staff should understand how a thesaurus is constructed, the design, terminology and features used. It is important to know how to adapt a thesaurus to suit one's specific information environment.

By the end of the course, participants will know how to:

- Apply the conventions of thesaurus construction.

- Use language effectively to produce a structured approach to a subject matter.

- Build or adapt an existing thesaurus.

- Evaluate the appropriateness of a thesaurus for use in a subject discipline.

Time management: introduction

A lot of time is wasted because of poor planning, failing to prioritise the workload, procrastination and responding to drivers like e-mails and telephone calls. Many people find it difficult to say 'no', thereby landing themselves with extra, often unimportant, work.

By the end of the course, participants will know how to:

- Manage their work activities.
- Prioritise their time and work.
- Handle interruptions.
- Overcome procrastination (deferring action).
- Say no to unreasonable or irrelevant requests.
- Manage other aspects of the work environment.

Training end-users: introduction

Many library and information staff are involved in training end-users. This may be helping a customer to locate a book, using a catalogue, or constructing an Internet search. Successful end-user training leads to an increase in the effective use of information within an organisation.

By the end of the course, participants will know how to:

- Identify and assess the training needs of the end-user (topic, level and depth).
- Design successful training sessions
  - training aims and outcomes;
  - use of different learning and teaching methods.
- Run a training session.
- Give instructions to users.

– one-to-one, small group and large group training.

■ Create audiovisual material by using different formats and technology.

■ Evaluate the training activity on successes, difficulties and future planning.

Training techniques: introduction

Training the trainer programmes have been developed by many organisations. These lead potential trainers through the successes and pitfalls of managing and delivering a training experience (course, workshop).

By the end of the course, participants will know how to:

■ Plan proactive training programmes.

■ Select and use a variety of training techniques – suitability, benefits, disadvantages.

■ Use the equipment and know what to do if a problem arises.

■ Develop training aids.

■ Deliver a training session.

■ Evaluate the training session.

■ Troubleshoot difficult situations and crises.

Web page design: introduction

Most organisations have their own website giving details about their role, function and services. While some libraries use a web page within the parent organisation's website, others have developed their own website. In the latter situation, librarians need to understand the concept of creating web pages and building websites.

By the end of the course, participants will know how to:

- Create HTML (or other language) pages using Notepad.
- Bring colour and images to web pages.
- Use tables to adjust layout.
- Use HTML editing software.
- Load the pages online.

Web and intranet searching: intermediate

Effective searching is a vital element in ensuring that users of websites and intranets can be certain that they have found all the relevant information that is available. The librarian needs to know how to select, install and implement the means to search for websites and intranets. Equally important is the ability to recognise the similarities and differences between searching websites and searching intranets.

By the end of the course, participants will know how to:

- Define the way in which a search engine works.
- Survey search engine suppliers.
- Make a business case for search.
- Search usability issues.
- Specify and select search engines.
- Implement website and intranet searches.

Web page design: intermediate

Web pages are only useful if they are maintained, regularly updated and give people the information they need to know. At the planning stage, web pages need to be well designed, pleasing to the eye, easy to read, form linkages and be navigable.

By the end of the course, participants will know how to:

- Form linkages to other pages and sites.
- Develop forms and frames.
- Use electronic publishing with PDF files.
- Incorporate images and scanned documents.
- Investigate web pages, meta tags and search engines.
- Maintain and update data.

Windows: introduction

Many people would benefit by getting a better understanding of the Windows environment. This would show them what it has to offer as well as the limitations on its use.

By the end of the course, participants will know how to:

- Open, close and minimise different packages and appliances.
- Use the toolbars, icons and programs.
- Set functions.
- Change the colour and appearance of the window.
- Use the help facilities.

Word processing: introduction

Much of the administration in a library relies on word-processing packages to perform housekeeping activities such as writing letters, form creation and keeping contact details.

By the end of the course, participants will know how to:

- Create and saved a word-processed document.
- Use different embellishments to enhance the document.
- Manipulate text using the cut, copy and paste facilities.
- Use the spellchecker and grammar facilities.

Word processing: intermediate

For many people being able to enhance and develop a word-processed document is a necessary part of their job. There may be a requirement to use tables, import images or paginate a report.

By the end of the course, participants will know how to:

- Refine a document by using headers, footers and pagination facilities.
- Import clip art and other images into a document.
- Customise toolbars.
- Set margins, tabs and page layout features.
- Use tables and columns.
- Use find and replace features to amend a document.

Word processing: advanced

Many advanced features within word-processing packages can be used to assist staff streamline the administrative functions of the library and information service.

By the end of the course, participants will know how to:

- Use the labels and envelope facilities and mail merge items.

- Use different styles, formats and templates.
- Create high-quality, professional documentation.
- Import other documents, images and items.
- Track a document and use auto-correct functions.

8

Informal non-conventional training techniques

Introduction

There are many ways to learn without having to go on a formal training course. These techniques are usually referred to as informal or non-conventional approaches to training.

The style or method suited to one individual may be quite inappropriate for another person. It is important to recognise which techniques are preferred by the trainee. A selection of different training methods is outlined below.

Mentoring

Definition

Chambers Dictionary (1994) defines the word 'mentor' as 'a wise counsellor: a tutor; a trainer; a more senior or experienced colleague appointed to help and advise a junior employee (business)'. A person who is under the guidance of a mentor is normally referred to as the 'mentee', although the term 'protégé' is sometimes used.

Clutterbuck (1991: 3) defines mentoring as a 'protected relationship in which learning and experimentation can occur, potential skills can be developed, and in which results can be measured in terms of competencies gained rather than curricular territory covered'.

Parsloe (1992) states that mentoring helps to 'support people to manage their own learning. In order to maximise their potential, and become the person they want to be.'

Background

Mentoring is reputed to have its roots in Greek mythology when Ulysses (Odysseus), entrusted his son, Telemachus, to the care of his trusted friend Mentor, 'to teach him everything' he knew.

Throughout history, mentoring has been used in various guises to train people. In the Middle Ages, a young man would be assigned as an apprentice to a master craftsman to learn a craft or trade. The older, more experienced artisan would guide the apprentice through his training, acting as mentor and passing on his knowledge and skills to the younger man.

In the 1960s, mentors were often seen as fearsome figures of ambiguous authority, who exacted power over their charges. Needing to be mentored was often seen as a sign of weakness, such as not being able to cope. By the 1970s, the mentor was a mixture of parent and peer, with the primary responsibility of being a transitional figure in a person's development. During the 1970s and 1980s, companies in North America began a rapid expansion of mentoring activities. It was not until the mid-1980s that mentoring, as a management tool, gained credence in Europe. By the 1990s, mentoring was being used as a career-progress technique to advance high-flyers or fast-track selected staff.

By the end of the twentieth century, mentoring was being used to help staff through periods of uncertainty and continuous change (Cannon and Taylor, 1994). Today, mentoring is seen as building a relationship that is founded on trust and mutual respect between the mentor and the mentee. It is a process that supports learning and development, enhances competency in the workplace and enables career development. On its own, mentoring will not cater for all the learning needs of the mentee. Mentoring, as a complementary tool, needs to be used alongside other training techniques, whether these are courses, shadowing or self-directed learning.

Types of mentors

Parsloe (1995) identified three types of mentor:

- *Mainstream mentor* – guides a person through various stages of their career. Many organisations have in place a formal mentoring scheme, where a member of staff is assigned a mentor with whom they can discuss issues and progress. The mentor supports and guides the mentee at various stages in their career. Mainstream mentoring is more about job satisfaction and problem solving than gaining promotion or achieving a qualification.

- *Professional qualifications mentor* – required by a professional association to guide a person through a professional qualification. In the UK, the Chartered Institute of Library and Information Professionals (CILIP) has a professional training scheme that requires each registered candidate to work with a mentor for the duration of the training period. Inexperienced mentors must complete a formal training session before working with candidates. Guidelines are available from *www.cilip.org.uk*.

- *Vocational qualification mentor* – required to guide a person through a series of competencies or to meet specific standards.

Vocational qualifications are sometimes regarded as the equivalent of 'modern apprenticeships'. The standards may be set by an organisation or through a national curriculum. Mentors work with trainees to ensure that the individual is able to meet the minimum performance criteria.

A mentee is likely to have a number of mentors throughout their working life. Equally, there will be periods where there is a total absence of a mentor. In some cases, a mentee may have more than one mentor at specific time in their career, for example, mainstream mentor and professional qualifications mentor.

It is important to recognise that not everyone is suited to be a mentor. A person should only become a mentor if they have the time to commit and willingness to see the process through. Many mentees see their mentors as role models, but the mentor is not expected to be the fount of all knowledge.

Mentor qualities

Mentors should have:

- confidence, trustworthiness, good rapport, respect for each other;
- responsibility to the mentee;
- time and commitment;
- a broad range of skills, experience and expertise
  - observation skills, to assess needs or recognise when help is needed;
  - listening skills;
  - questioning skills;
  - negotiating, persuading and influencing skills.

Mentors should:

- provide reassurance, be supportive, non-threatening;
- be perceptive, sympathetic, empathetic, caring;
- be able to provide information;
- help to identify problems and find solutions;
- give direction, improvement to performance;
- understand the learning styles and how people receive ideas;
- review and reflect on learning;
- provide meaningful feedback and evaluation of performance;
- be constructive, encouraging and motivational;
- maintain a professional relationship, with conduct and manner appropriate to role;
- be flexible – available when needed – there at appropriate times.

Mentoring process

The normal practice in the workplace is to have a mentor from outside the immediate environment, for example, from another section or department. This means the mentor can view things more objectively, particularly if there is conflict. At times, the mentor may be required to enter into discussion with the mentee's line manager over issues raised. The mentor must ensure that such actions lead to improvement rather than alienation or interference.

Mentoring is about creating relationships through the sharing of knowledge, experiences and expertise. It assists with the individual's learning, growth and development. In a world where people feel 'battered' by the pace of change, it helps them to cope with a changing environment. Mentoring does not give advice but seeks to endow the individual with the wisdom needed to find a solution or make an informed decision.

Mentoring goes through four phases:

- *Establishing the relationship*: Finding out about each other, building rapport and respect, deciding how to progress, what is required of each other.

- *Main activity*: Learning/growing together, problem solving, meeting at regular intervals, being available when needed, offering support, nurturing the mentee, confidential discussions, building confidence, giving and receiving constructive feedback.

- *Ending the relationship*: Recognise when the time has come to bring the process to a formal but positive end; part on good terms; recognise the natural point of departure (where there is no more to be gained at this time or level); outline the values and experiences gained on both sides. The ending can be forced if the mentor becomes emotionally involved or is no longer able to cope with the mentee.

- *Informal relationship*: Normal to have some interaction, even if at a distance, e.g. an occasional query, seeking reassurance, updating; ensuring mentee moves on to next stage in development.

Clutterbuck (1991) uses the MENTOR mnemonic to summarise the mentoring relationship:

- *Manage* the relationship;
- *Encourage* the mentee;
- *Nurture* the mentee;

- *Train* the mentee;
- *Offer* mutual respect;
- *Respond* to the mentee's needs.

Mentee preparation checklist questions

Before the first session, the mentee should consider what they want to get out of the meeting. A suggested list of questions is given below:

- What do I want to get from the whole mentoring experience?
- What do I what to discuss in the first session?
- What do I expect to get from the first session?
- What kind of help do I need now?
- What are my priorities?
- What do I want to know about my mentor?
- What will my mentor want to know about me?
- How will we build trust between us?
- What can I offer the mentoring process, e.g. enthusiasm, honesty?
- What are my strengths and weaknesses?
- Where do I see the threats and opportunities?

For both parties, mentoring always stays on a professional level, that is, retaining rapport but remaining objective. Should the relationship become personal or emotionally involved, it must be terminated. There are no rules to stipulate how long the mentoring process will last, but it does have a finite end, a time at which the relationship should be dissolved. The timeframe, which could be anything from three months to two years, is dependent on a host of factors, such as meeting the mentee's requirements, going beyond mentor's scope, or successful completion of a qualification. Successful mentoring offers the following benefits:

- For the mentee:
  - greater understanding (of work role);
  - self-confidence;
  - learning outcomes;
  - developing personal skills;
  - career development;
  - problem solving;
  - reflection and feedback;
  - gaining skills, knowledge, experience and expertise.
- For the mentor:
  - business functions;
  - personal and job satisfaction;
  - role enhancement;
  - expansion of skills repertoire;
  - personal self-development;
  - career enhancement;
  - continuous learning;
  - discovering and developing talent.
- For the organisation:
  - improve skills bank – trained staff;
  - development of organisational culture;
  - learning organisation;
  - effective management development;
  - positive learning experience;

- empowered status;
- improved morale and motivation.
- For the profession:
  - managed career development;
  - growth in skills and knowledge;
  - gaining experience and expertise;
  - improved networks;
  - meeting standards and competencies;
  - improved status.

Coaching

The importance of coaching was recognised by Socrates, who used it as a learning technique with his students. Coaching is closely allied to mentoring, and some see it as an interchangeable term. Mentoring and coaching employ similar techniques, such as listening, observing and questioning skills. However, there are a number of differences between the two methods. Whereas the mentor is normally a person outside the immediate work environment, the coach is usually the line manager. Unlike mentoring, coaching has no finite end as it is a continuous learning process. In the workplace, coaching is normally on a one-to-one basis although there are times when the whole team may be coached. Many parallels are drawn with the coaching activities seen in sport.

Definition

Chambers Dictionary (1994) defines the term *coach* 'as a private tutor, a professional trainer in athletics, football'.

John Whitmore, a leading figure in both sport and management training defines coaching as 'unlocking a person's potential to maximise their own performance. It is helping them to learn rather than teaching them ... Good coaching is a skill, that requires a depth of understanding and plenty of practice if it is to deliver astonishing potential' (Whitmore, 1992).

'Coaching is directly concerned with the immediate improvement of performance and development of skills by a form of tutoring or instruction. Mentoring is always one step removed and is concerned with longer-term acquisition of skills in a developing career by a form of advising and counselling' (Parsloe, 1992).

Performance coaching

Coaching is about target setting, working in bite-size chunks towards a specific goal. Successful coaching will improving the individual's performance, helping them learn new skills, gain experience and consider long-term career prospects. To be effective in achieving these goals, the individual is forced to move outside their comfort zone. At this point the trainee may require mentoring, helping them to identify issues and problem areas and think through options or solutions.

The enemy within

Gallway (1975) was one of the first to recognise that the 'enemy within' is often the biggest obstacle to success, that the 'opponent within one's own head is far more formidable than the one on the other side of the net'. For many years, teaching people new skills focused on a linear plane of knowledge (technique) and experience (fitness). It was in the latter part of the twentieth century that *attitude of mind* was recognised as being crucial to an individual's development (see Figure 8.1). Only by developing a culture of self-belief, self-awareness and self-confidence can the enemy within be overcome. By working on all three elements, a successful coach will help a person exceed their own limitations and take them beyond what they believe or expect of themselves.

Role of the coach

The coach often takes an objective overview to assess performance. The next step is to analyse what has to be done to maximise competence. The expert coach does not give advice or orders, nor tell the trainee what to do. Rather they use observation, questioning and listening skills to help the learners explore and find out for themselves. Both coach and trainee share in the responsibility for the individual's development.

The relationship between coach and trainee is built around honesty and openness. The coach must be forthright in feedback on performance, praising what has gone well, and assessing how to improve less satisfactory outcomes. The coach enables the trainee to learn from good and bad

Figure 8.1 Whitmore's coaching triangle

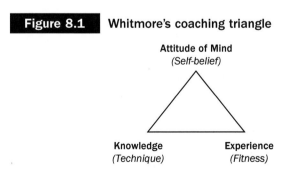

© Whitmore, J. (1992) *Coaching for Performance: A practical guide to growing your own skills*, p. 23.

experiences, working on weaknesses and threats, and extending strengths and opportunities. Like the mentor, the coach is often seen as a role model. Ultimately, good coaching will take the trainee beyond the limitations of the coach's own knowledge, skills and ability.

Key elements in coaching are:

- *responsibility*: taking ownership;

- *self-motivation*: willingness, opportunity, drive, self-esteem;

- *awareness*: clarity of perception.

The main responsibilities of a good coach are to:

- give uninterrupted time and commitment to the trainee;

- establish rapport and build confidence;

- motivate the trainee to succeed and achieve results;

- reinforce learning and give praise when appropriate;

- help the trainee to identify and solve problems;

- recognise when the trainee is having difficulty coping
    - understand body language and behaviours;

- give praise, encouragement and support;

- challenge and stretch the individual;

- clarify discussions by using listening, questioning and observation skills;

- know when to use other training techniques to advance the trainee's learning
    - recognise the trainee's preferred learning style;

- provide sound feedback in a non-judgmental way;

- focus on future developments and career opportunities;

- check back on how the trainee is feeling;

- remain objective.

The qualities, skills and attributes of a coach:

- Being:
  - attentive;
  - authoritative;
  - detached;
  - empathetic;
  - interested;
  - knowledgeable;
  - perceptive;
  - reflective;
  - supportive;
  - a talent-spotter;
  - trustworthy.
- Having:
  - awareness;
  - credibility;
  - experience;
  - patience;
  - technical expertise.

Coaching process

The whole coaching process is driven by asking questions so that trainee becomes more aware of their capabilities, experiences and expertise. Each part of the process focuses on clearly defined tasks or specific activities and uses the KISS-KIL principles – keep it simple and short, keep it lean. The process is illustrated in Figure 8.2.

Figure 8.2   Coaching process

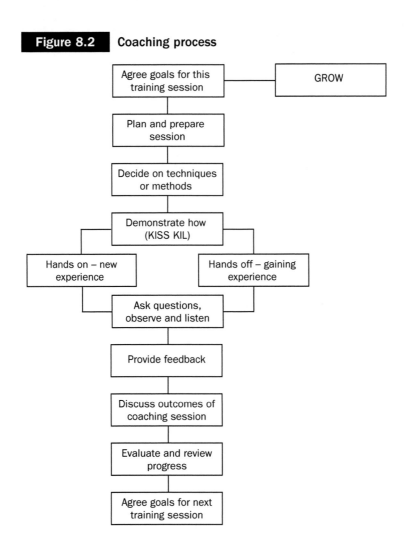

In the initial questioning phase, Whitmore (1992) suggests using the four GROW headings to clarify what has to be achieved.

- Goal setting:
  - What do you want to achieve this session?
  - What do you want to achieve overall?

- What are your short and long-term targets?
- Using SMART, PURE and CLEAR objectives.

■ Reality:

- Exploring the current situation.
- Remaining objective.
- Eliminating distortions.
- Overcoming inner obstacles (enemy within).

■ Options:

- What alternatives are available and feasible?
- Which approach or style should be used?
- What barriers need to be overcome?
- Coping out of the comfort zone.

■ What, when, who?

- What will you do to convert discussion into action?
- Who can help you?
- Who will hinder your progress?
- How long will each phase take you? What are the timescales?

Successful coaching offers the following benefits:

■ For the trainee:

- improved performance;
- better understanding of work role;
- self-confidence, more self-awareness;
- personal achievements;
- developing practical skills;
- problem solving;
- reflection and feedback;
- gaining knowledge, experience and expertise.

- For the coach:
  - personal and job satisfaction;
  - role enhancement;
  - expansion of skills repertoire;
  - personal self-development;
  - learning from trainee;
  - motivational;
  - greater creativity;
  - developing talent;
  - flexibility and adaptability.
- For the organisation:
  - improved performance and productivity;
  - meeting competency standards;
  - improved relationships;
  - positive learning experience;
  - improved morale and motivation;
  - workforce fit for purpose.
- For the profession:
  - advancing career development;
  - growth in skills and knowledge;
  - gaining experience and expertise;
  - growing the individual;
  - meeting standards and competencies;
  - status recognition.

Coaching can be labour-intensive, requiring a lot of time and commitment from the line manager. It focuses on improving performance and developing skills. The coach provides feedback to the trainee, concentrating on extending strengths and developing weaknesses. Coaching often involves other training techniques such as mentoring.

Listening skills

An integral part of the mentoring and coaching process is to develop expert listening skills. This is primarily helping someone to help themselves. There may be many reasons why someone needs to talk to another person, for example, they may have made a wrong decision, be unable to resolve a problem, or be unsure how to progress. The mentor or coach needs to recognise the signs when the trainee is experiencing difficulties, such as their body language or being out of character, withdrawn, emotional, angry, upset or irrational. Effective listening means the mentor or coach must be able to:

- *evaluate*: based on judgment;
- *interpret*: based on analysis;
- *support*: based on reassurance;
- *probe*: based on 'tough' questioning;
- *understand*: based on thought and feeling.

Jo-Hari window

In order to talk openly, the trainee must have absolute confidence and trust in the mentor or coach. The Jo-Hari window indicates what is known about the behaviour and intentions of an individual in two dimensions. At the beginning of a relationship, each will know little about the other. As the relationship develops, each party begins to learn more about the other person and the 'open' window grows. No matter how trusting the relationship, there will always be areas that the trainee is unwilling to discuss, which stay firmly within the 'hidden window'. Likewise, there will always be some limitations to understanding the behaviour of others. The Jo-Hari window at the beginning of the relationship is illustrated in Figure 8.3.

Questions asked at this stage of he relationship include:

- What do I know about this person?

- What do I not know about this person but may be able to find out?

- What do I know about this person that the individual does not know?

- What does this person know about themselves but will not share with me?

Figure 8.4 illustrates the Jo-Hari window once the relationship has been extended.

Figure 8.3 Jo-Hari window at the beginning of the relationship

Beginning of relationship	Known to self	Not known to self
Known to others	OPEN	BLIND
Not known to others	HIDDEN	UNKNOWN

Figure 8.4 Jo-Hari window – extending the relationship

Established relationship	Known to self	Not known to self
Known to others	OPEN	BLIND
Not known to others	HIDDEN	UNKNOWN

LUNSIE principles

Listening goes through three stages, referred to as structured intervention:

- *define*: presenting a problem or situation;
- *describe*: exploring the situation;
- *decide*: seeking solutions.

LUNSIE breaks this into the stages of listen, understand, no advice, summarise, information and encourage:

- Listen:
  - hear what the person is saying – this may be more than the spoken word;
  - indicate that you are listening
  - maintain eye contact;
  - recognise body language and non-verbal signals;
  - manage the silence – let the trainee think.
- Understand:
  - be clear about the problem or issue;
  - ask open questions – who? what? when? why? how?
  - empathise and sympathise;
  - ask about feelings, e.g. how did you feel about that?
- No advice:
  - do not give advice – you may not have the full picture, and the advice you give could be wrong;
  - the trainee will blame you if the advice is wrong;
  - try to ascertain what the trainee knows already;
  - does the trainee know how to solve the problem but is looking for guidance?
  - help the person to find a solution.

- Summarise:
  - rephrase to ensure data has been assimilated correctly;
  - take notes (as long as the trainee consents);
  - ask closed questions to clarify issues, e.g. have I understood correctly?
- Information:
  - ascertain what the trainee knows already;
  - give adequate information to fill knowledge gap;
  - do not impose own views or opinions;
  - draw out learning experiences;
  - identify details that help the individual, e.g. who else might be able to help?
- Encourage:
  - seek to explore further and motivate;
  - encourage dialogue and discussion;
  - channel knowledge and ability to achieve the 'task';
  - time needed – do not hurry.

An important element of the listening process is to *manage the silence*. Allow the trainee time to reflect and think. The silence may be uncomfortable so do not answer your own questions or leap in with your own suggestions (which may be wrong).

Summarising

At the end of the discussion:

- go back over main points;
- summarise what has been done, said, achieved;
- check back with individual before proceeding;

- note agreed actions – who is doing what, follow-up actions.

Problem solving diamonds

It is important in any mentoring or coaching session to recognise when the trainee is troubled. What appears on the surface to be a problem may not be the primary reason for the difficulty. The problem-solving diamonds model (Figure 8.5) helps to identify the facts and problems, then seeks to suggest solutions and consider the consequences.

In trying to identify the underlying problem, the mentor/coach asks a series of questions to establish the facts. Having gleaned this evidence, it is possible to unravel the cause of the problem(s). The mentor/coach then works with the trainee, looking at all the options that would help to solve the problem(s). In considering a solution, another problem may be identified, in which case both parties need to revisit the facts.

By the use of questions, the trainee is encouraged to find their own solutions and think about the consequences, thus negating the need for 'advice'. The outcome does not mean that the perfect solution has been found, but having considered all the options, the trainee is then able decide the

| Figure 8.5 | Problem-solving diamonds |

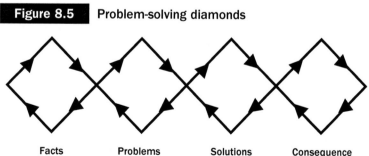

Facts   Problems   Solutions   Consequence

Adapted by The Scout Association from an original model developed by Relate.

best course to take. People often stop at the solutions phase without considering the consequences of their actions, thereby creating a new problem or perhaps exacerbating an already difficult scenario.

The trainee should be doing at least two-thirds of the talking, while the mentor or coach should speak only to ask questions, clarify issues, summarise understanding or reflect on feelings. It is useful to remember the phrase 'I have two eyes, two ears and one mouth so that I can see and hear twice as much as I talk'.

Questioning skills

To get people talking, the mentor or coach needs to use a variety of methods. At the beginning of the discussion, general questions should be asked to put the person at ease. The mentor or coach must be clear what they want to get from the trainee and the session. It is therefore necessary to think about the questions to be asked in advance, especially those of a sensitive nature or delicate matter. What is a serious problem to the trainee may be a trivial matter to the mentor/coach. The relationship can be destroyed by the mentor/coach being over-critical, aloof, belittling or laughing at the trainee.

Throughout the discussion, the mentor/coach must remain in control of the situation. They must be able to handle a range of emotions, such as defusing anger, channelling aggressions felt by the trainee, and coping with withdrawal symptoms.

The mentor/coach needs to:

■ Keep the questions simple to understand

  – no ambiguity

  – how else could the question be phrased?

- Think about responding to statements
  - how will you handle a surprise reply or something unexpected?

- Allow the person time to think
  - never ask a question then answer it yourself.

- At appropriate moments ask the trainee to reflect on feelings and emotions
  - how did that make you feel? how are you feeling now?

- Know when to ask open or closed questions
  - know when to probe deeper.

- Use closed questions, i.e. those requiring yes/no answers
  - to clarify – is this correct, have I understood?
  - interpretative – redefining, paraphrase then check back.

- Use open questions to find out more detail:
  - who? what? where? when? how? why?
  - encourage the trainee to think, examine, explore and analyse.

- Use probing questions to dig deeper
  - do not become intrusive;
  - do not become threatening.

Perhaps the best way to sum up questioning is to remember Rudyard Kipling's tale of the Elephant Child from the *Just So Stories*:

> I kept six honest serving men,
> (They taught me all I knew);
> Their names are What and Why and When
> And How and Where and Who.
> I send them over land and sea,
> I send them east and west;

But after they have worked for me
I give them all a rest.

The wrong question (or right question in the wrong place) can cause resentment, demotivates the trainee and may damage or destroy the relationship.

Observation skills

Observation skills involve verbal and non-verbal activity; these may be the tone of voice, gestures, facial expressions and feeling of emotions. Most of the observing we do will include sight and sound as the predominant faculties, such as how a person speaks on the telephone or how the individual interacts with a colleague. There are at least 50 ways to say a statement such as 'I love you'. Much depends on the intonation of the voice and the expression of sentiment coupled with non-verbal actions. These reactions and responses tell us if someone is happy, fearful, nervous, sad, bored, frustrated, angry, caring, helpful or sarcastic.

For many mentors and coaches, observation skills are about keeping a watchful eye on the trainee to ensure that they are coping during times of stress. This means watching the person at work, making both mental and written notes about the individual's performance. The trainee's confidence is likely to grow if the observer, as part of a routine practice, makes several visits to the workplace so they do not feel intimidated. During these sessions, the coach/mentor will discuss some of the observations made and await responses and reactions from the trainee. What reactions and responses are seen may not be the person's 'normal' behaviour, and assessment can only be made over a prolonged period. The outward expression, or the person's behaviour at a given time, may influence the expected result. This complex combination of behaviour, reaction and activity may help the mentor/coach to observe how a person is performing, and whether the trainee is struggling to achieving an acceptable minimum standard.

Observation may be formal or informal. In a formal situation, both parties are aware of the activity, the trainee is conscious of the mentor/coach watching them execute a task, whether a specific exercise, simulation or presentation. Formal observation will form a major part of the coaching activity. However, people become self-conscious when a video camera, camcorder, camera, microphone or Dictaphone is introduced into a meeting or training session. This may alter behaviour or influence the outcome of a discussion, for example, someone refuses to speak. Attitudes may vary from Hollywood superstar in-waiting to total recluse.

Informal observation is undertaken without the individual's conscious knowledge. It may be done over a period of time, for example, several visits, friendly mentoring chat. The individual may be observed from a 'remote' location, for example, video conferencing, surveillance, or without the candidate being aware of the watching brief.

A technique used by a number of mentors during a 'difficult listening' session is to observe the trainee, then subtly mirror the body language, for example, trainee crosses arms, mentor crosses arms, trainee leans forward, mentor leans forward. This must be done in a non-intrusive way and without mimicking. Subconsciously it helps the trainee to relax and open up. The mentor/coach can then use the SOLER technique to encourage the trainee further.

SOLER looks for approachability and an indication of feelings:

- Smile;
- Open;
- Lean forward (slightly);
- Eye contact;
- Relaxed.

Any observation activity has to be done in a non-threatening way, and must respect cultural differences, such as hand gestures or bowing. Much depends on how well the trainee and mentor/coach know each other but proximity plays an important part in a relationship, for example, invading personal space. For some training activities, the coach may need to touch the trainee or come close to demonstrate a procedure. The experienced observer will know whether the trainee feels comfortable or threatened.

Generally, the balance between physical distances and comfort zones can be summarised as:

- *Intimate*: comfort zone = 0–45 cm (0–18 inches)
- *Personal*: comfort zone = 45–120 cm (18–48 inches)
- *Social*: comfort zone = 120–365 cm (4–12 feet)
- *Public*: comfort zone = Over 365 cm (over 12 feet)

Listening, questioning and observing offer the following benefits:

- For the trainee:
  - people feel more responsibility for something they have helped to create;
  - greater commitment to completing a given task and reaching a desired outcome;
  - self-development, taking responsibility for learning;
  - feeling of comfort.

- For the mentor/coach:
  - steering trainee in the right direction;
  - effectively utilising the skills, experiences and expertise;
  - building trust and confidence;
  - opportunities to talk and share;
  - feeling of achievement or satisfaction.
- For the organisation:
  - effective feedback helps to improve performance and productivity;
  - improved quality of life in the workplace;
  - improved relationships;
  - better use of people, time, resources, and more creativity.
- For the profession:
  - growing personally and professionally
  - experiential learning;
  - meeting the required standards;
  - expansion of skills, knowledge and expertise.

As well as giving feedback, the mentor/coach should be seeking reflective comments from the trainee. This is needed to confirm understanding, clarifying points and provide a breathing space. At the end of the process, the mentor/coach must ensure that there are no loose ends. Action must be taken to redress any outstanding issues and to ensure that all follow-up actions have been initiated.

The mentor/coach should be able to view a person holistically, from a distance of impartiality, but be able to make a rational judgment about the individual's strengths and weaknesses. The mentor/coach is not there to cast moral judgment, they are there to help, support and guide the trainee – helping to improve performance to meet agreed minimum standards. All observations should be positive and helpful, offering constructive feedback and justifying why a particular action was taken. Finally, as a role model, the mentor/coach is being observed by the trainee.

A selection of other training methods

There are many other non-conventional ways of being trained.

Job shadowing

Shadowing allows a trainee to learn about a job or task by following and observing a more experienced person around the workplace. During the shadowing period, the trainee is encouraged to ask questions and make notes. This technique is often employed when a person is new to the organisation, a member of staff is about to retire, or at a senior level as a buffer zone between or during a crossover period. The period of shadowing is dependent on the level of seniority and complexity of the work. It may last one day or for several weeks.

On the job training

On the job training is sometimes referred to as 'sitting next to Nellie'. The derivation of the term 'sitting next to Nellie' is uncertain. It has been suggested that during seventeenth-century Britain, 'Nellie' was used to refer to someone of low birth or a lowly servant (a skivvy). Anyone one new to the factory or kitchen would be shown how to do the job by 'sitting next to Nellie'.

On the job training is one of the most widely used methods to develop staff skills. It differs from shadowing in that the trainee has an opportunity to practise the taught techniques. The training is normally done on a one-to-one basis.

'Nellie' is usually seen to have acquired the knowledge and expertise needed to perform a task to a satisfactory level. For instance, someone dealing with interlibrary loans will know which forms to use and understand the process to obtain the required items. Drawbacks to this method of training may be that Nellie is not competent to train other people, or has inculcated bad habits that are then passed on to the trainee.

Secondment

Secondment is when a person is detached from their regular place of work and temporarily assigned to another section of the establishment. This may be used in project work, during staff absence, promotion or periods of change. It is completed over a set period, for example, six months, after which the employee returns to their normal place of work.

Job rotation or cross-training

Job rotation is used as a means to provide variety and experience. The individual is moved through a series of assignments designed to increase their exposure to a range of operations, activities, competences and environments. Job rotation is seen to boost innovation by enabling staff to apply knowledge and skills to a number of tasks. Cross-training promotes a better understanding of what other people do and how each job contributes to the function of the section or organisation. Having staff who can work in a number of roles or positions creates a more flexible workforce.

Project work/steering committees

Project work or being part of a steering committee are useful ways to gain practical experience in the workplace. This process involves a group of people working together to complete a piece of work. During the development phase, the individual may work on their own activity (specialist area of work) but they are an integral component in the finished article. The process often requires the preparation of progress and final reports outlining the results or findings. This type of training activity introduces the individual to project management, team working, leadership and such things as managing meetings.

9

Facilitation

Introduction

In a training context, facilitation is the art of being able to work with small and large groups to maximise learning and development, by putting people at their ease. The facilitator is usually an outside mediator who is the 'objective eyes' of the group(s) helping to maintain balance and order.

Facility – facile – easy to accomplish; easy; working with ease.

Facilitation is concerned with helping people to:

- encourage exploration, dialogue, discussion, exchange;
- communicate thoughts, views or visions to achieve a common goal;
- engage in processes that are new, difficult or changing;
- capitalise on their skills, talents and potential;
- direct skills, knowledge and ability in the correct direction to achieve task;
- work at a pace to achieve the task;
- draw out learning experiences;
- ascertain the knowledge of individuals;
- assimilate collective intelligence of group.

A facilitator needs to respect and understand the values, beliefs and behaviours that occur in groups. Values are what people consider to be important. The level of importance is likely to vary between group members. Beliefs are what people think is true and this becomes their reality. Behaviours are observed action of what people do. These are normally driven by specific values and beliefs.

Task, individual and group

John Adair's group approach model (also known as TIG or action centred leadership) concentrates on three crucial elements: task, individual and group. This is normally portrayed as three overlapping circles (Figure 9.1) (Adair 1997a, 1997b).

The model implies an understanding of the environment in which the facilitator is working. Before beginning on any training or group work, the facilitator needs to be clear about each element:

- Task:

    - What is the purpose of this task? Why are we doing this?

    - What is the task? Is it one task or many tasks?

Figure 9.1   Group approach model

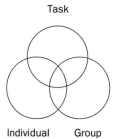

Task

Individual   Group

© Adair, J. (1998) *Leadership Skills.* Management Shapers series, London: CIPD, p. 16.

- – What is the importance of completing the task or tasks? What happens if the task is not completed? What impact will this have on the group and the individual?
  - – Will the group members have the necessary skills to complete the task?
  - – What are the time constraints?
- ■ Individual:
  - – What do I know about this person?
  - – What are their strengths, skills, expertise, ability and capability?
  - – What fears, worries or anxieties will this person have?
  - – Will this person cope with the assigned task?
  - – What will motivate this person?
  - – What effect will they have on the other group members?
  - – How will this activity help the individual to grow and develop?
- ■ Group:
  - – What are the group dynamics?
  - – What is the culture of the group?
  - – Does the group possess all the skills needed to achieve the task?
  - – How will the members interact?
  - – Will they be able to work together to achieve the task?

Group dynamics

Every person belongs to a group, whether formal or informal, well defined or vague. A group consists of two or more people who meet together for a specific purpose. The effectiveness of the group relies on how it interacts together – to achieve a task, to resolve a conflict or to improve performance.

To be productive, a group needs to work together. By its nature, the group is unpredictable and sometimes unstable. Effectiveness is achieved by a conscious effort of the members, who work hard to create agreement and harmony within the group. For the group to work effectively, each member must pass through three behavioural stages of self-realisation:

- dependent (selfish);

- independent (self-centred);

- interdependence (selfless).

To achieve a higher performance or better output, the group must work in an interdependent mode. Interdependence relies on effective relationships between the members. Productivity relies on healthy debate, constructive conflict, creativity and innovation while making best use of the group members' skills and knowledge. Facilitation is used to promote synergy within the group.

Perhaps the best-known approach to group dynamics is the model developed by Tuckman (1965). Tuckman identified four stages of group development, usually referred to as the, 'Orming Model – forming → storming → norming → performing (see Figure 9.2). He updated his model in the 1970s to include a fifth stage, mourning.

- Forming – arriving:
    - group comes together for the first time
    - uncertainty and anxiety, period of testing;
    - needing to understand the group's purpose
    - uncertain of task or members;
    - unknown resources and skills of group members;
    - different ideas, different directions.

Figure 9.2   Tuckman's 'Orming Model

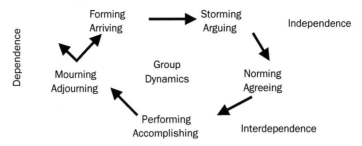

- Storming – arguing:
  - finding out about group members;
  - identifying what individuals expect of each other; how they should work together;
  - conflict and competition within and outside of group;
  - uncertainty of own position;
  - cliques – individual does not feel a part of the group;
  - not meeting expectations; needing to feel important.
- Norming – agreeing:
  - if the group are to work together they must start to resolve differences;
  - negotiating to establish ground rules, preparing group's charter;
  - establishing harmony and trust;
  - commonality of purpose;
  - group still unsure of how they should work together.
- Performing – accomplishing:
  - working with all group members to achieve productivity and effectiveness;

- activities that will accomplish task, producing the output, interdependence attainment;
- defining clear roles.
■ Mourning – adjourning:
- group feels a sense of loss when it is dispersed or a member leaves.

Group history

Some questions for the group:

■ Why was the group formed?

■ What is its purpose?

■ How long ago was it formed? (Age is measured from the time the last person joined or left the group.)

■ What is it membership?

■ What is the culture of the group?

■ What skills does each member possess?

■ What are the similarities or differences between the members?

Any changes to the group dynamics – member leaving, new person joining – will affect the performance of the group. Each stage will be revisited with the changing formation of the group. Groups sometimes get stuck during the first three stages. There will be peaks and troughs as the group struggles to emerge from each stage to achieve effectiveness. It may be painful at times. The facilitator's role is to gently steer, coerce or push the group through each stage. Much effort will be required to get the group to the performance stage.

Group relationships

Relationships within the group occur at different levels:

- facilitator – group;
- facilitator – individual members;
- individual member – other individuals;
- individual member – group.

At some stage, the group will probably reject the facilitator (seen to be the outsider, or interloper).

Facilitator's role

To be effective the facilitator must possess some, if not all, of the following qualities, attributes and skills and must be able to:

- treat everyone with respect and make everyone feel important – do not embarrass the individual;
- remain objective and impartial;
- motivate the individual and the group;
- drive group toward the desired outcome or goal;
- encourage participation;
- clarify tasks;
- define members' roles;
- plan ahead by making adequate preparation and be ready to troubleshoot;
- help group to make decisions;
- arbitrate and help to resolve conflict;
- ask questions that may be awkward or difficult for the group;

- think before intervening;
- monitor what is happening.

Ground rules for good facilitation

No two groups work alike; their composition, culture and skills will vary. It is up to the facilitator to decide what will inspire and motivate the group to produce results. At the first meeting, the facilitator should use an icebreaker or energiser to help group members find out about one another. The next stage of facilitation starts by asking a comfortable opening question, e.g. tell me six things about yourself. A selection of icebreakers or energisers is given in Appendix D.

The facilitator needs to ascertain whether any hidden agendas, issues or potential areas of conflict require addressing. How will the group and its members work towards the goal? What set of actions or tools, exercises or interventions will help the group progress? What is the best way to use the skills, expertise and knowledge of the group? The opening session should use 'inclusive' training methods to start discussions, for example, brainstorming, buzz groups, round table.

Questions

The facilitator needs to indicate where and when questions will be taken, for example, any time, at the end of a session, at the end of the morning. A useful quote to start a training sessions is:

> There is no such thing as a dumb question. The only bad question is the one you do not ask. (Professor Tom Cyrs, New Mexico State University)

Setting ground rules

At the outset the facilitator needs to set the ground rules and agree these with the whole group. For example, these might include:

1. Only one meeting at a time – no secondary discussions.
2. Record discussion then sort the wheat from the chaff.
3. Provide clarity over confusion.
4. Facilitator to intervene in cases of conflict.
5. Encourage participation by all group members.
6. Offer help and support to other members.
7. Turn off mobile phones and pagers.
8. Leave all emotional baggage at the door.
9. Confidentiality – all discussions remain within the room.
10. Respect for other points of view.

To help with cohesion, there should be a set of rules for each group, i.e. a group charter.

Actions by the facilitator

At all times the facilitator must remain objective and impartial, for example, not interjecting with personal opinions, not taking sides. It is up to the facilitator to help ease the process for the individual and group. More will be achieved if the participants feel they are in a 'caring' environment. The facilitator must ensure that the group follows the 'rules' and that only good social behaviour is acceptable. Open-ended questions should be asked to stimulate discussion or seek clarification. The facilitator must encourage each person to be fully involved in the session and respond positively to each contribution, even if the comments are not helpful, for example, 'thank you, that was an interesting point; we may be able to discuss this later'. It is the facilitator's responsibility to provide any background information needed to complete a task or to enable the knowledge gathering exercise to take place. Occasionally the facilitator may need to rise above the details of the debate to keep the group on track, for example, assisting with decision-making, enabling the group to reach conclusions or complete tasks.

Observation and reflection

The facilitator must observe the group and its members on two levels. The first is to watch and note what is being said and done. This information can be made available to the group if it needs help. The second level accumulates, digests, interprets the signs and detects patterns in the group's behaviour and activities. At appropriate times, the facilitator may wish to share these observations with the group. This process is known as *reflection*. Reflection helps the group to focus its thoughts or brings it back to the task. Although the group may reject the facilitator's observations, it is likely to use some of the information and then draw its own conclusions.

Conflict situations

At some stage, the facilitator will be faced with a conflict situation. This arises where people appear to have different desires, needs, wants, opinions or beliefs. This often happens at the storming stage where individuals are still uncertain of their roles, or are trying to exert their authority. Some people, like the agents provocateur, actively seek out arguments and find the clash exciting and stimulating, while others seek to avoid any form of disquiet or unsettling behaviour, preferring to withdraw from the group altogether.

Every group will experience conflict at some time in its life, whether this is mild or severe. Depending on how conflict is handled, it can be healthy and creative, or demotivating and destructive. Conflict can be due to a clash of roles or of personalities. For the individual, conflict arises when they feel threatened, insecure, undermined or belittled. This happens when the individual believes that they are losing something they value, such as ideals, standards, aspirations, reputation, status or self-esteem.

There are many reasons why conflict occurs. It may be an ongoing problem or an instantaneous reaction to a given situation. In some circumstances, it could fester under the surface for a while, and then explode without warning. On other occasions, the trigger may be a minor irritation, which clouds or influences someone's view or perspective.

Recognising conflict

The following are signs of conflict:

- arguments between group members holding opposite or differing viewpoints;
- disruptive behaviour – when one person ruins the activity for the remaining members;
- domineering or overwhelming loud and intimidating characters within the group;
- quiet, reserved and uncooperative people, withdrawn from the group;

- when emotions are highly charged;
- when controversial or difficult subject matter leads to tense atmosphere;
- when loyalty is tested, split or difficult to accept; experience of betrayal;
- breakdown in communications.

Three roles may be identified in dysfunctional groups:

- *Victim*: Feels pain, discomfort, feeling of loneliness or isolation.
- *Persecutors*: Uses bullying tactics to harass and oppress the victim.
- *Rescuer*: Tries to help the victim by intervening.

It has been known for the persecutor to unite with the victim and then turn on the rescuer, so that the rescuer becomes the new victim (the enemy of my enemy is my friend).

Handling conflict

The facilitator can take a number of actions to mediate and ease a conflict situation. Throughout the conflict situation, the facilitator must stay neutral by not taking sides, while thinking of ways to reduce tension. Next, the background to the problems needs to be recognised and understood. To do this, the facilitator needs to clarify and summarise their understanding of situation. As emotions will be tense, the facilitator must handle the situation sensitively, checking on feelings and, when necessary, create a cooling-down period. On some occasions, the conflicting parties may have to be separated from the group. This action, in itself, will affect the group dynamics.

Conflict resolution steps

Steps to be taken by the facilitator:

- Meet in a mutually acceptable environment.
- Acknowledge the problem and focus on the issue.
- Discuss matters privately and work with each person; listen and talk with each individual
  - observe verbal and non-verbal communications;
  - manage the silence.
- Seek to express and clarify the differences
  - agree on commonalities;
  - not proving the other person wrong.
- Forget about egos and accept personality differences
  - be willing to compromise if this eases tension.
- Be direct but choose your words carefully.
- Keep your own emotions in check.

Taboo

The facilitator must not:

- get out of their depth or become embroiled in the battle;
- be seen to be taking sides;
- allow the situation to undo any good work created up to that point;
- sit passively by and hope it will go away – react at the appropriate time;
- rush the group through a period of conflict;
- have winners and losers.

Should the facilitator not be able to cope, then the matter must be referred to another person or professional help should be sought, e.g. counselling.

Outcome

■ Agree to resolve conflict and find means of achieving harmony.

■ Use the best method to find a solution (no right answer)

   – negotiate for an acceptable settlement;

   – compromise and foster cooperation.

■ Make deliberate efforts to maintain mutual respect.

■ Ensure health of the individual, health of the group, health of the team.

Summary

Not all conflict is bad or unhealthy. All groups need some form of conflict to stay alert. Conflict can make some groups become more inventive, creative or innovative. Remember that all conflict can be managed – it takes time and patience. In any conflict situation, it is important to keep a sense of perspective and the *test of three* should be applied – will this conflict matter in three minutes, three hours or three days?

There will be times when groups easily pass through all stage of the 'Orming process. At other times, the individuals or group may struggle to cope with the dynamics. Effective utilisation of the skills, experiences and strengths of the group and members will help them through the most testing situations. Satisfaction can be achieved where all members of a group have participated and the desired outcome has been achieved. All learning experiences have highs and lows, peaks and troughs. Facilitating a group can be a testing and rewarding experience, but like any art, it requires practice.

10

Academic, professional and vocational learning

Introduction

There are many opportunities available to staff to gain academic, professional and vocational qualifications. In educational terms, these training activities are subject to formal curricula set by national organisations such as universities and professional associations. The award of such qualifications is normally subject to examination or formal assessment. Although some professional societies operate on a global scale, the range of qualifications available varies between countries. Within the higher education sector, international schemes exist that give equal status and recognition to university degrees taken in other countries. Some professional associations have reciprocal agreements recognising each other's academic and professional qualifications, e.g. the Chartered Institute of Library and Information Professionals, American Library Association, and Australian Library and Information Association recognise each other's qualifications.

Learning opportunities

There are many learning opportunities where information professionals may acquire knowledge and update their skills:

- *Academic qualification*: leads to an educational certificate, diploma or degree. A mark of distinction conferred by universities and colleges, either earned by examination or research or granted as a mark of honour. University curricula are normally subject to a validation process to ensure standards and robustness of the courses. National bodies (government or agencies) carry out the quality assurance process through inspections and monitoring.

- *Professional qualification*: successful completion of professional exams, portfolio or report submission leads to a professional qualification such as Membership or Chartership status. Completion of the qualification confers or confirms titles, rights or privileges, e.g. post-nominals such as MCLIP. As well as requiring membership of the professional association, admission to the professional register is fee-based. Membership is controlled by professional ethics, which means that professional qualification can be taken away, e.g. due to failure to pay professional fees or subscription, gross misconduct or action that bring the profession into disrepute.

- *Vocational qualification*: pertaining to, concerned with, or undertaken in preparation for a trade or occupation. Occupational standards are governed by competency-based criteria requiring assessment and verification. The qualification is usually modular based and takes the form of units of competence based on occupational roles and responsibilities. Candidates must be able to demonstrate that they have the underpinning knowledge and competence across a range of services and activities.

Successful completion of the course leads to a certificate of competence. Standards are set by national bodies or government agencies.

- *Occupational training*: work-based activities to meet defined competency levels relevant to needs of organisation; learning objectives and application are specific to the work environment. It is normally the line manager's responsibility to ensure that the staff have the necessary training to complete their work.

- *Development*: self-directed learning is a key element in the professional and personal growth of the individual; this encourages the development of potential talents and ambitions. It is the individual's responsibility to make the most of opportunities to update skills and knowledge.

- *e-Learning*: facilitated and supported through the use of information and communications technology; e-learning can cover a spectrum of activities from supported learning and blended learning, to learning that is entirely online. Courses and other training activities are undertaken via the Internet or with the use of technology (CDs, DVDs, video, satellite broadcasting, interactive television, webcam). Students submit work as interactive forms, attachments, discussion forums or other technological means. Quality assurance measures are put into place to ensure that submission of material is the candidate's own work. Many distance learning courses lead to academic qualifications, e.g. degree, diploma.

- *Distance learning*: a course of learning that is geographically remote from the educational establishment. Tuition takes place by means of video conferencing, televised broadcasts, webcams, postal correspondence or telephone link. Students complete the studies using workbooks, videos, CDs and DVDs. Sometimes the student is required to attend a residential weekend or local centre. Students are supported by a personal tutor (telephone, e-mail). May lead to an academic qualification.

- *Sponsorships and bursaries*: a number of organisations offer the chance for individuals to extend their learning through exchange visits (to other organisations or countries), travelling scholarship, completion of a piece of research or attendance at conferences or training courses. The sponsorship or bursary is usually done through open competition when an applicant is nominated for the award. An example is the Special Libraries Association (SLA) that sponsors the SLA Europe Information Professional Awards. The winner receives expenses-paid trips to conferences and meetings; in return, the winner is expected to give presentations and write for the association's newsletter. Sponsored candidates are normally expected to submit a report or other piece of work on the learning experience.

Assessing prior learning

Adults usually bring a great deal of experience and prior knowledge to any new learning situation. It is important that the trainer acknowledges the adult's understanding and experiences of the topic and that they help the adult learner to see the connections between earlier learning experience and new information which helps validate the prior learning. This is referred to as accreditation of prior learning (APL) or accreditation of prior experiential leaning (APEL). Using APL or APEL the trainer is able to find out what the adult already knows, whether it is relevant and to identify gaps in learning.

Assessment is the process of documenting, in measurable terms, knowledge, skills, attitudes and beliefs.

- Assessment of learning questions:
  - how you are to going to 'test' the learning?
  - what constitutes underpinning knowledge and know-how?
  - what are the minimum competencies required for this job or situation?
  - how will you identify the gaps or weaknesses that need to be addressed?
- Competence:
  - a standard required for an individual to perform a specific job;
  - the quality of being adequately or well qualified physically or intellectually;
  - the quality of being competent or capable of performing an allotted function;
  - a specific range of skill, knowledge or ability.
- Accreditation:
  - the act of granting credit or recognition, especially with respect to an institution that maintains suitable standards;
  - the process in which certification of competency or authority is presented.
- Validation:
  - certifies conformance to a standard;
  - the act of judging or assessing a person, organisation, situation or event;
  - to prove something to be sound or logical;
  - to ascertain the truth and authenticity of an organisation's or a person's capability.

Assessments can be classified in many different ways:

- Formative assessment:

    - continuous throughout a course or project;
    - used to aid learning;
    - teacher, peer or the learner provide feedback on a student's work;
    - not necessarily used for grading purposes.

- Summative assessment:

    - carried out at the end of a course or project;
    - in an educational setting, summative assessments are used to assign students a course grade or pass mark.

- Objective assessment:

    - a form of questioning which has a single correct answer; includes true or false answers, multiple choice, multiple response and matching questions;
    - popular with use of online assessment (this form of questioning is well-suited to computerisation).

- Subjective assessment:

    - subjective assessment is a form of questioning which may have more than one current answer (or more than one way of expressing the correct answer);
    - subjective questions include extended-response questions and essays.

- Criterion-referenced assessment:

    - candidate is measured against defined (and objective) criteria;
    - used to establish a person's competence (whether candidate can do something);

- the best-known example is the driving test;
- does not vary from year to year (unless the criteria change).

■ Norm-referenced assessment:
  - is not measured against defined criteria;
  - standards may vary from year to year, depending on the quality of the individual;
  - assessment is relative to the student body undertaking the assessment;
  - used as a way of comparing students;
  - entrance tests (e.g. to schools or universities) permitting a fixed number of students to pass, rather than relying solely on academic ability.

■ Formal assessment:
  - usually a written document, such as a test, exam, quiz or paper;
  - given a numerical score or grade based on individual's performance.

■ Informal assessment:
  - does not contribute to a individual's final grade;
  - usually occurs in a more casual manner, including observation, inventories, participation, discussion, peer and self-evaluation.

Building a professional portfolio: some pointers

Taken from a presentation given to healthcare librarians in London, November 2006.

Introduction

Your portfolio is about I, me, my, mine. It is not about your line manager, we, our, them or other people's work. Your portfolio is a record of the activities that you have completed against specific criteria. Your portfolio is a folder or file in which to record your reflective account, evidence, forms and other details as per criteria, contents page and index. *Chambers Dictionary* (1994) provides the following definitions:

> *Portfolio*: Noun: A case or pair of boards for holding loose papers, drawings; a collection of such papers, e.g. drawings or photographs put together as examples of a student's work. Origin: Italian *portafogli(o)*, from Latin *portare* to carry, and *folium* a leaf.

> *Evidence*: Noun: That which makes anything evident; means of proving an unknown or disputed fact; support (e.g. for a belief); indication; information in a law case; testimony; a witness or witnesses collectively. Verb: To make evident, apparent or visible; to attest or prove; to indicate. Origin: Latin *evidens, -entis*, from *e* from, and *videre* to see.

Reflective writing

There are two types of reflective writing: descriptive and analytical/evaluative. In a descriptive account, you tell a story. It is a narrative account of your experiences, e.g. how you handle interlibrary loans and discussing problems that you have dealt with. For the analytical and evaluative account, you build and think around your experiences. It is a dialogue or argument that critically examines events and activities by identifying shortcomings, successes and solutions.

The process of reflective writing starts by keeping a diary or logbook. The purpose is to make sense of events and activities that have occurred over a period time, e.g. six months. From the recorded facts, you develop a personal hypothesis about why something happened (or did not happen). You then extract the pertinent details, e.g. trends, problems, achievements, that will form the basis of your account.

Reflective writing critically examines values, assumptions, behavioural patterns, professional decisions, lifestyle and skills. It can reveal a number of things, such as discrepancies, intentions or imbalances, for which you will need to seek clarification. It is important to retain a certain amount of detachment when compiling your reflective account as the process requires a level of self-criticism, which, if not handled correctly can lead to self-destruction instead of self-confidence.

Reflective writing needs to convey the message that you are competent, have the underpinning knowledge and have fulfilled all the requirements. The account must have a structure that is systematic, logical and well ordered. Reflective practice involves constructive criticism; this means writing in a positive way about negative experiences, e.g. negative experience = positive action. In this way, dilemmas turn into challenges, struggles turn out to be breakthroughs, problems are converted into successes and frustrations develop into illumination.

There is an art to writing a critical appraisal, but by using the appropriate analytical and evaluation tools, this process becomes easier. Such tools include PEST or SWOT analysis, the problem-solving diamonds model (Figure 8.5), and reviewing what went well, what difficulties occurred, why, and what the future action plan might be.

Evidence

Any evidence presented must be your own work and must meet the criteria. The evidence you present needs to demonstrate:

- competence;
- professionalism;
- quality over quantity;
- adequacy over insufficiency.

In addition, it must be:

- selective and discerning;
- reliable – credible, accurate;
- valid – relevant;
- current (within 1–3 years);
- transferable (can be used in other sections, sector or disciplines);
- authentic – i.e. *your work.*

Evidence comes in many forms:

- appraisal;
- articles or publications;
- certificates;
- charts, maps, diagrams;
- correspondence;
- display;
- e-mails;
- evaluation forms;
- handouts;

- leaflets;
- manual instructions;
- observation;
- photographs;
- posters;
- presentations;
- programmes;
- reflective accounts;
- reports;
- taped discussion;
- videos, CDs, DVDs;
- web pages;
- witness testimonies.

Feedback

Most schemes (vocational or professional) require candidates to have a mentor or supervisor. This is the person who supports and guides the candidate through the process. The role requires the mentor or supervisor to ask questions, give praise and provide feedback on performance. Has this met the criteria? These are the good points, What further work needs to be done?

Portfolio presentation

Remember the portfolio is about *you* and *your* work. Much depends on the scheme as to how the portfolio is presented so check back on the requirements. If the criteria state a maximum 500-word reflective account, do not submit a script of 400 or 600 words. If you are asked for a handwritten manuscript account, do not send in a word-processed report.

Your portfolio is a working document, so it does not have to be 'perfect'. If it is not obvious from a piece of evidence that it is your work, then highlight your contribution or write a short annotation.

There are issues around confidentiality. This may be governed by privacy laws or an organisation's code of practice. It is normally recommended that personal names are anonymised and work titles used instead, e.g. deputy library manager. In some instances, names may need to be deleted or blanked out, e.g. minutes of meetings, correspondence, case histories.

Have you:

- checked your contents against the criteria;
- included all the areas required
  - include background description of service as required;
- included documents for which you are personally responsible
  - highlight or annotate the text to show your contribution;
- included a bibliography or references (correctly cited);
- cross-referenced the text and evidence;
- numbered the evidence (sectional, sequentially, chronologically);
- paginated each page;
- provided a contents page/index;
- proofread (not just spell checked)
  - get someone else to proofread.

Does your portfolio demonstrate:

- a sense of professional growth;
- a sense of a personal perspective;
- what you have learnt from experience;
- an awareness of the wider information community;
- evidence of membership of professional groups/committees;
- a good presentation indicative of professionalism.

Assuming your portfolio has met all the criteria, it is now ready to be submitted for assessment. Hopefully, the end result will be a positive outcome with the achievement of a professional or vocational qualification.

Examples of reflective practice

Descriptive

Criteria: Obtain information for users

My main job is looking after the enquiry desk. I am responsible for issuing and discharging books, hastening overdues and general enquiries. I also deal with interlibrary loans.

When a request is received for a document, I check the catalogue to see if it is held in stock. If it is, I look to see if it is on the shelf or booked out to a user. If it is available, I issue the item to the user. If it is with another reader I put a reserve notice against the name for when it is returned. I recall an item if it is overdue.

If the item is not held in stock, I arrange for it to be borrowed from another library. The library is part of the SWELL regional interlibrary loan scheme. I check the holdings from the regional catalogue to see which library holds the item. I complete the forms and send them off to the participating library. This can be faxed to some libraries; others will accept an online e-mail, while a few still prefer the form to be posted. If the participating library has the item in stock it will be sent to me via the document delivery service. If they are unable to help, I will try some of the national lending schemes. I ensure that all requests are filed. I keep the user informed of what has happened to the request.

Analytical and evaluative

Criteria: Assess service performance to meet user need

Since reorganisation, the number of people making personal visits to the library has fallen. The changes and restructuring have resulted in the new client base being geographically remote from the centre. To ensure that the library was meeting users' needs I sent a questionnaire to heads of departments in each branch for distribution to their staff. The questions asked were:

- What was done well in the way of service provision?
- What services should continue?
- What service should cease (or be reduced)?
- What services needed changing or improving?
- Were there were gaps in service provision (e.g. subject areas, material)?

Forty-five questionnaires were returned (30 per cent of the number sent out). I analysed the results. These revealed that most people were satisfied with the library and that it appeared to meet the users' needs. Suggestions were made for improvements to stock (subject matter and recommended purchases) and a request made for an e-mail alerts service to be instigated. The content and way in which the current awareness bulletin was circulated needed urgent review. More development is needed on the intranet and the library web pages – including new additions to stock, searching instructions, links to other sites, better interfaces for the book catalogue and journal holdings. All the recommendations are now under investigation. I will send a report on the findings of the survey, to the Chair of the library committee before the next meeting.

Much as I miss the personal contact, a further analysis showed that more people were using the library services but by telephone, fax and e-mail. The conclusions reached indicated that the library continues to provide a valuable and relevant service to its users.

Example of professional scheme

Chartered Institute of Library and Information Professionals (CILIP) – UK

CILIP is the leading professional body for librarians, information specialists and knowledge managers. There are around 23,000 CILIP members working in all sectors. CILIP is committed to the development and promotion of the highest levels of professional practice. CILIP operates a framework of professional qualifications – these are Certification, Revalidation, Chartership and Fellowship. Application for all qualifications is by the preparation and submission of a portfolio. This is a rigorous process that can be readily accommodated into existing staff appraisal schemes and other development activities. The focus at all levels is on evidence-based practice ensuring that staff reflect on their own learning and applications of new knowledge and skills that are specific to their workplace. Anyone wishing to complete a CILIP qualification must be a fully paid-up member of the Institute. Permission has been given by CILIP to include copies of the Framework of Qualifications© in this book (see Appendix E).

Certification

Certification recognises the contributions made by library and information staff working in a para-professional capacity. Throughout the training period, the candidate is supported at local, regional and national level. This takes the form of training courses, networks, reading lists, discussion lists and meetings. Although a qualification in its own right, the Certification Scheme enables successful candidates to progress to Chartership Membership through work-based learning.

Applicants for Certification must have been:

- *Category 1:* Employed in library and information work for five years or more (full-time equivalent), or

- *Category 2:* Employed in library and information work for two years (full-time equivalent) and have participated in work-based training or other staff development (e.g. National Vocational Qualifications Levels 2 or 3, City and Guilds).

Candidates are required to submit a portfolio that includes a 500-word evaluative reflective account and supporting evidence. Candidates must be able to:

- evaluate personal performance;

- evaluate service performance;

- reflect on training and development;

- demonstrate an understanding of the importance of continuing professional development (CPD);

- appreciate the role and contribution of library and information services in the wider community.

Two Chartered Members from a CILIP assessment panel, assess the portfolio against the criteria. The pairing of assessors changes with each portfolio. The assessors must not know the candidate.

Successful completion of the Certification leads to the Associateship award and entitles the candidate to use the ACLIP post-nominals. A copy of the Certification framework is given in Appendix E.

Chartership

Chartered Membership (MCLIP) is the second highest professional qualification awarded by CILIP and is considered the 'gold standard' for the information professional. It is recognised throughout the world. Chartered Membership is not an academic award but a recognition of the highest standards of professional practice and a commitment to undertake continuing professional development. CILIP recognises the dynamic nature of the information environment and the need to offer flexible routes to the MCLIP qualification. Throughout the training period, the candidate is supported at local, regional and national level. This takes the form of mentoring, training courses, networks, reading lists, discussion lists and meetings.

Applicants for Chartership must hold:

- academic degree in librarianship, information science or a related area; or
- certification (and working at a professional level);
- exceptional circumstance may be made for candidates holding other qualifications who can demonstrate extensive LIS professional development.

All candidates are required to have a mentor from the CILIP register of mentors. (Mentors are required to complete a mentoring course.) The mentor and candidate agree the personal learning plan and meet on a regular basis to discuss progress.

Candidates are required to submit a portfolio that includes a 1,000-word evaluative reflective account and supporting evidence. Candidates must be able to:

- critically reflect on personal performance;
- critically reflect on service performance;
- analyse personal/professional development in relation to work role and development activities;
- demonstrate a breadth of professional knowledge and understanding of wider professional context;
- show evidence of participation in mentor scheme.

Two Chartered Members from the Chartership Board assess the portfolio against the criteria. The pairing of assessors changes with each portfolio. Assessors must not know the candidate.

Successful completion of the Chartership leads to the Chartered Member award and entitles the candidate to use the MCLIP post-nominals. A copy of the Chartership framework is given in Appendix E.

Revalidation

Through the code of professional practice, all Chartered Members have a commitment to improving and enhancing professional practice. Many regulatory bodies require formal revalidation. The CILIP revalidation scheme offers such formal recognition. Continuous professional development underpins revalidation. It is important that practitioners demonstrate that they are regularly updating their knowledge and skills. Chartered Members can use a wide range of activities to gain official recognition of their professional commitment and achievements. The scheme operates on a three-year cycle.

Throughout the three-year revalidation period, the candidate is supported at local, regional and national level. This takes the form of mentoring schemes, training courses, networks, reading lists, discussion lists and meetings.

Candidates are required to submit a portfolio that includes a 500-word evaluative reflective account and supporting evidence covering the three-year revalidation period. Candidates must be able to:

- critically evaluate the personal learning outcomes from training and development activities;
- show increased competence in range of professional/ management skills;
- demonstrate evidence of continuing professional development;
- provide evidence of professional involvement and awareness through reading, participation, courses, conferences.

The portfolio is assessed by two Chartered Members from the assessment panel, who examine it against criteria. The pairing of assessors changes with each portfolio. The candidate must not be known to assessors.

On successful completion of the three-year revalidation period candidates receive a Certificate of Revalidation.

Fellowship

Fellowship is the highest professional qualification awarded by CILIP. It signifies that a Chartered Member has applied an increasing level of professionalism through personal professional practice and through the contribution made to the profession at large.

Applicants for Fellowship must have:

- six years at Chartered Membership MCLIP level; or
- two successful revalidation cycles (equal to six years).

Candidates are required to submit a portfolio that includes a 500-word evaluative reflective account and supporting evidence. Candidates must be able to demonstrate evidence of:

- substantial achievement in professional practice;
- significant contribution to profession;
- active continuing professional development.

Two Chartered Members from the Chartership Board assess the portfolio against the criteria. The pairing of assessors changes with each portfolio. The candidate must not be known to assessors.

The achievement carries the right to the designation Chartered Fellow and the right to use the post-nominals FCLIP, Fellow of the Chartered Institute of Library and Information Professionals.

For further details on the professional qualifications for CILIP please contact:

Qualifications and Professional Development Department
Chartered Institute of Library and Information Professionals
7 Ridgmount Street, London WC1E 7AE, United Kingdom
Telephone: +44 (0)20 7255 0500
Fax: +44 (0)20 7255 0501
Textphone: +44 (0)20 7255 0505
E-mail: *quals@cilip.org.uk*
Website: *www.cilip.org.uk*

11

Conclusion

Today's work environment is constantly changing and putting demands on staff to keep pace. To respond to these changes, the workforce needs to be flexible and adaptable. Organisations want people who can help to grow the business and develop the services required. This means having a highly-trained workforce that is competent, capable and motivated to succeed.

Personal success can only be achieved where the individual takes responsibility for their own vision, plans, actions, progress, achievements and learning. Self-development is a continual process and successful people seek to develop and improve themselves continually. 'Self-development helps us to recognise that change is a natural and inevitable part of our working lives, stimulating us to be aware of our own role in responding to it' (Megginson and Whitaker, 1996). To ensure that skills stay relevant for each new set of circumstances, the librarian must constantly re-evaluate their assumptions and behaviours.

Jobs should have sufficient challenge to utilise the full abilities of the employees. All staff need to have personal development plans – each person must know where they are going and what has to be done, by when. An important part of this process is to receive feedback on how well, or badly, the individual is performing, and to identify gaps in knowledge.

In the twenty-first century, there is a need to think differently about the way in which people undertake training and development. This recognises the importance of identifying the preferred learning style and then tailoring the training to the individual. Learning is most effective when it reflects the way the individual wants to learn. Once a developmental activity has been completed, the individual must be given the opportunity to implement learning and put the training into practice.

There are many reasons why training, development and learning are important:

- creating a competent workforce with defined minimum standards;
- encouraging professionalism at all levels helps staff to appreciate their role;
- increasing the understanding of the organisation's aim, user needs and service development;
- creating dialogue between colleagues, users and other agents;
- identifying gaps to be addressed, acquiring new skills, responding to the changing environment, updating and refreshing skills;
- providing opportunities for constructive feedback;
- providing support through a variety of means, such as coaching, mentoring, courses, on the job training;
- helping to change behaviour and attitudes of the individual and in the workplace;
- providing opportunities to change or improve working practices;
- improving motivation and performance;
- maintaining and improving a quality service.

The global society does not recognise nor respect boundaries. Areas that were once the domain of the librarian have been encroached upon by other sectors, faculties, groups and professions. Library and information staff will need to have experience, expertise and proficiency in traditional, electronic and transferable skills. The key skills required in the twenty-first century include strategic thinking, managing change, financial management, customer satisfaction, communications, decision-making, as well as understanding the role of IT, information and knowledge.

Appendix A
London Library and Information Development Unit training needs analysis document

Staff training and development needs

The London Library and Information Development Unit is updating its database of training needs. With your line manager, please identify what training or development you will need over the next 12 months, indicating the level and best method of meeting those needs. Please supply additional details if an area has been overlooked or a particular skill not accommodated in the listing.

Please use the following codes to indicate the type, methods, urgency and level of training required.

Category:

- APV: Academic, Professional, Vocational
- EBH: Evidence-Based Health Care
- ITC: IT Software Packages, Applications, Systems
- LIS: Library and Information Skills; Records Management; Information Consultancy

- MST: Management and Soft Skills; Training
- OTH: Other Skills, e.g. Health and Safety

Methods:

- APV: Academic, Professional, Vocational Courses
- CSE: Formal Courses (e.g. 1 or 2 days; 10 weeks)
- DSL: Distance Learning, Correspondence Courses
- ITW: At the Bench, On the Job, Sitting Next to Nellie; In the Workplace
- MEN: Mentoring, Coaching or other Support
- OTO: One to One Sessions
- OTD: Other Training Options, e.g. night school
- PFO: Portfolio, Self Taught
- PTP: Prescribed Training Programme, e.g. Chartership
- SLM: Seminars, Lectures, Conferences, Workshops, Meetings

Urgency:

- *Critical (C)*: Within next 1–12 weeks
- *Urgent (U)*: Within next 3–5 months
- *Essential (E)*: Within next 6–9 months
- *Desirable (D)*: Within next 12 months

Level:

- *Beginner (B)*: Little knowledge, expertise or understanding
- *Intermediate (I)*: Some knowledge, expertise and understanding
- *Advanced (A)*: Lot of experience and expertise. Looking at specialist areas

Evidence-based health care

EB01: ADEPT Principles
EB02: Biomedical Information on the Internet
EB03: Cochrane Database
EB04: Critical Appraisal Techniques
EB05: Medical Databases
EB06: Medline Database
EB07: Quality Filters
EB08: Searching Techniques and Database Interrogation
EB09: Training End Users
EB10: User Questionnaire
EB30: Other EBHC Skills (Please give further details)

Information technology

IT01: Automation Skills
IT02: Database Construction
IT03: Databases (Please specify)
IT03: DB Textworks
IT04: Desktop Publishing
IT05: E-mail Systems
IT06: Graphics
IT07: HTML, JAVA
IT08: Internet / Super Highways
IT09: Intranets
IT10: Online Communications
IT11: Programming
IT12: Retrospective Conversion
IT13: Search Engines
IT14: Spreadsheets (Please specify)
IT15: Systems Administration
IT16: Web Page Design
IT17: Windows Environment

IT18: Word Processing (Please specify)

IT30: Other IT Skills (Please give further details)

Information consultancy

IC01: Information Consultancy

IC02: Information Evaluation

IC03: Information Flows and Processes

IC04: Information Strategy

IC05: Knowledge Management

IC06: Legal Issues and Licensing

IC07: Management Information Systems

IC08: Marketing

IC09: Policy, Procedures and Practices

IC10: Research Methods

IC11: Setting up a Library and Information Service

IC12: Service Level Agreements

IC30: Other Information Consultancy Skills (Please give further details)

Library and information skills

LI01: Abstracting

LI02: Accessioning and Processing

LI03: Audio Visual

LI04: Cataloguing and Classification

LI04: Collection Studies

LI06: Copyright and Legal Information

LI07: Current Awareness and SDI Profiling

LI08: Indexing

LI09: Interlibrary Loans

LI10: Library Housekeeping

LI11: Publishing and Editing

LI12: Reference Work

LI13: Serials Management

LI14: Statistical Analysis

LI15: Stock Selection and Acquisition

LI16: Thesaurus Construction

LI30: Other Library and Information Skills (Please give further details)

Management and soft skills

MS01: Business Development Plans

MS02: Change Management

MS03: Client Liaison / Customer Care

MS04: Coaching and Mentoring

MS05: Communication and Listening Skills

MS06: Decision-Making and Problem-Solving

MS07: Employment and Legal Issues

MS08: Finance and Budgeting

MS09: Interpersonal Skills

MS10: Job Evaluation

MS11: Managing a Resource

MS12: Managing Staff

MS13: Managing a Service

MS14: Meetings and Committee Work

MS15: Negotiation Skills

MS16: Performance Appraisal

MS17: Personal Development Plans

MS18: Project Management

MS19: Public Relations

MS20: Quality Management

MS21: Recruitment, Selection and Interviewing

MS22: Report Writing

MS23: Team Leadership and Motivation

MS24: Time Management

MS30: Other Management Skills (Please give further details)

Professional and vocational

PV01: Chartership
PV02: Certification
PV03: NVQ Information and Library 2
PV03: NVQ Information and Library 3
PV04: NVQ Information and Library 4
PV05: NVQ Records Management 2
PV05: NVQ Records Management 3
PV05: NVQ Records Management 4
PV30: Other Professional and Vocational (Please give further details)

Records management

RM01: Archive Administration
RM02: Auditing
RM03: Conservation and Preservation
RM04: Data Protection
RM05: Documentation Control
RM06: Filing Systems
RM07: Records Management
RM08: Records Security
RM09: Retention Scheduling
RM10: Storage
RM30: Records Management Skills (Please give further details)

Training and development

TD01: Courseware Development
TD02: Directing a Training Experience
TD03: Facilitation Skills
TD04: Instruction Skills

TD05: Managing a Training Experience

TD06: Personal and Professional: Development

TD07: Presentation Skills

TD08: Public Speaking

TD09: Training the Trainer

TD30: Other Training and Development Skills (Please give details)

Other skills

OS30: Other Skills not covered elsewhere (Please give further details)

Individual training needs

Name:

Post:

Location:

Tel No:

Fax No:

E-mail:

These training needs have been agreed with the line manager

Line Manager Signed:

Date:

Subject Area	Criticality					Methods	Level		
	C	U	E	D			B	I	A

Appendix B
Example of a staff
appraisal form

There is no perfect layout to the appraisal form – it is dictated by organisational policy but must be reviewed and updated as to reflect changes.

Name:

Post:

Grade:

Organisation:

Tel/Fax no:

E-mail:

Academic qualifications:

Professional or vocational qualifications:

Date of appointment to post:

Work profile/job description:

1

2

3

4

5

6

Are the scope and purpose of the
appraisee's job clear?   Yes/No

Does profile match the work undertaken?   Yes/No

If No, please specify the differences:

Competence levels – self-assessment:

Skill categories	1	2	3	4	5	6
Administration and organisational skills (record keeping, filing)						
Business skills (finance, budgeting, business plans)						
Dress code (uniform, appropriateness)						
Health (fitness for work, sickness)						
Interpersonal skills (effective communications, team player)						
IT skills (software packages, use of applications)						
Library and information skills (primary functions)						
Management skills (leadership, managing a resource)						
Mental ability (ability to reason, judgment)						
Productivity (quality of work; quantity of work)						
Soft skills (coaching, customer liaison)						
Technical skills (written work, numeracy)						
Time management (time keeping, punctuality)						
Overall rating of ability to do the work						

Key to performance:

1. None: Skills are not, at present, relevant to the task.

2. Poor: Struggles to complete or achieve the task.

3. Adequate: May need help or assistance to complete the task.

4. Satisfactory: Completes tasks in hand; effective in work role.

5. Good: Executes tasks well.

6. Excellent: Authoritative, innovation, high level of expertise and experience.

Review of last 12 months

Training and development completed in the last 12 months (topics and usefulness):

Progress towards achievement of objectives/competencies/ achievements of the last 12 months:

Difficulties and obstacles encountered in the last 12 months (and reasons):

What steps were taken to overcome these obstacles?

Expectations for the next 12 months (desired outcomes or achievements):

Skills that the appraisee feels are not used:

State here how the objectives will be achieved, what methods will be used and how will the successes or difficulties be measured?

Objectives	Measurement	Review date
1		
2		
3		
4		
5		

Competencies are the skills, knowledge and attributes needed for effective performance in the job. Competencies are generic to the profession/organisation.

Competency area	Standard required
1	
2	
3	
4	
5	
6	
7	

Personal development programme/training and development requirements for the next 12 months:

Topic	Level	Method	Urgency	Expected outcome
1				
2				
3				
4				
5				
6				
7				
8				
9				
10				

Methods:

- APV: Academic, professional, vocational e.g. higher education degree.

- CSE: Course, either internal or external.
- OTJ: In the workplace, e.g. on the job; sitting next to Nellie.
- MEN: Other support, e.g. mentoring, one-to-one.
- ELD: e-learning, distance learning or similar programmes.
- OTM: Other training methods, e.g. self-taught.

Level:

- B: Beginner – Little knowledge, expertise or understanding.
- I: Intermediate – Some knowledge, expertise and understanding.
- A: Advanced – Lot of experience and expertise. Looking at specialist areas.

Urgency:

- C: Critical within next 3–5 months.
- E: Essential within next 6–9 months.
- D: Desirable within next 12 months.

Expected outcomes (examples):

- Filling skill deficiency: Greater understanding of work role.
- Updating skills: Better organisation of work.
- Developing new skills: Improved performance.

Updating on appraisal of work – Setting mid-term or half-yearly dates

Comments by Appraisee:

Comments by Appraiser:

Signed (Appraiser)   Dated:

Signed (Appraisee)   Dated:

Review 3 months

Review 6 months

Review 9 months

Appendix C
Examples of covering letter and CVs

Your Names

Address

Tel No

E-mail

Mr/Ms/Dr ...

Company Name

Address

Post/Zip Code

Date

Job Ref ...

Dear Mr/Ms ...

Application For >Post >

Please find enclosed my application/CV for >Post Title> as advertised in *'Publication' and Date*

This is what I have to offer ... (don't repeat all CV details). Work experience

This is how my application fits the job description

This is why you should employ me.

State that you are willing to learn, keen and enthusiastic.

Available for interview. Look forward to hearing from (Company Name). Please contact me if you require any further information to support this application for (Repeat Post title).

Yours sincerely (if addressed to individual)

Yours faithfully (if addressed to Sir/Madam)

Yours truly

Your Signature

Your name

Qualification Post nominals (e.g. PhD; MA; MCLIP)

Helen Du Bois PhD MA BA MCLIP
23 Lilac Gardens, Windmill Green, Hampshire SO1 10XZ
Tel: 042 121 5863, E-mail: *hdubois@blanketshirecc.co.uk*

Professional, academic and vocational qualifications

PhD MA BA MCLIP
Certificate in Research Methodology; NVQ A1 and IV; 3 'A'
Levels; 10 GCSEs

Professional background

Information Consultancy; Information Science; Archives
Administration; Records Management

Professional competence

- Management of Library and Information Centre
- Management and training of staff – professional and non-professional
- Maintenance of company databases for housekeeping and information retrieval
- Organisation and management of company documentation (records management)
- Writing profiles, business plans, aims and objectives
- Liaising with staff, management and external authorities
- Organisational skills, time management and project management skills
- Ability to work – autonomously; as part of a team
- Familiar with project and committee work
- Able to meet deadlines and work to tight schedules
- Good office practice and keyboard skills

Work experience

Head of Library and Information Service (2000 to date)
Blanketshire County Council

Responsible for all information work in Chief Executives Office and Legal Services Division. Jurisdiction over Legal Information Centre (Law Library, Central Filing Systems and Modern Records, Archives). Handling all enquiries relating to Data Protection and Freedom of Information. Liaising with 22 departments and agencies.

Research Librarian Social Services (1998–2000)
Blanketshire County Council

Creation of Social Services Library – covering bookstock, journals, government publications. Setting up databases to support work of Social Services (Child Care, Elderly, Family). Literature searches on clinical issues such as non-accidental injuries. Ensuring compliance with Data Protection. Liaising with other departments.

Healthcare Information Development Unit (1996–1998)
Project Coordinator – Training and Development

Responsible for the development and competency of the library and information services staff working in the National Health Service in London and the Home Counties. Activities include – implementation of the progressive modular training programme; undertaking a training needs analysis; and organising CPD events. NVQ Assessor for ILS and records management; supervision of candidate completing professional Chartership of CILIP.

Centre for Medical Research (1993–1996)
Information Services Officer

Overseeing Information Services Department, Retrospective conversion of CMR Library onto Libertas: downloading, conversion and editing of records. Data Protection Officer. Chair of the Office System Working Party; Newsletter Editor. Member of Quality Steering Group.

Professional membership

Chartered Institute of Library and Information Professionals
Chartership Board Member
Member Personnel and Training Group; Career and Development Group
Records Management Society

Education

University of Swanick	PhD	1998–2000
University of Swanick	Certificate in Research Methodology	1998–1999
Edexcel	NVQ Assessor and Internal Verifier	1997–1999
University of Swanick	MA Information Management	1993–1994
University of Burridge	BA (Hons) Library Studies	1990–1993
NWKCT College	A Levels	1989
Kent School for Girls	GCSE	1987

PhD Thesis 'Investigating the need for national policy for LIS in the 21st century'

Interests

Full clean driving licence
First aid certificate
Sport: Team sports; racket sports, swimming, fitness training
Other: Bird watching and gardening

SCOTT PATERSON STEVENSON BSc MSc
21 PROVENMILL ROAD, BLACKHILL, GLASGOW G1 2AB
Tel: 0141 9753 2864; Mobile: 07779 792 999; E-mail: *SPS@sportsmedicineresearch.org*

Appointment

Assistant Librarian, Sports Medicine Research Library

Academic achievements

BSc, MSc; Working towards Chartership

Current employer

Sports Medicine Research: 2003 to date

Responsibilities

Conducting literature searches on all aspects of sports medicine
Training staff how to use the in-house and commercial databases
Maintenance of IT systems
Secretary to Library Committee
Deputising for Library Manager
Enquiry work
Supervision of two part-time library assistants

Work experience

Gap Year travelling and working around America and Australasia (1998)
Camp America – Running sport activities for children
Working as an diving instructor, Australian Gold Coast
Researcher, Hospital Library, Melbourne, Victoria

Education

2003	Strathclyde University Dissertation – Comparative analysis of medical literature to support the use of cardiac rehabilitation fitness programmes	MSc in Information Science
1999–2002	Loughborough University	BSc Sports Science
1996–1997	Blackhill College of Technology	Scottish Highers
1991–1995	Botley Valley School	GCSEs

Interests

Sport: Rugby (Scrum Half); Scuba Diving; Climbing and Fell Walking

Driving licence

First Aid Instructor

Appendix D
Examples of icebreakers and energisers

The icebreakers and energisers outlined below can be changed to suit local circumstances or adapted to become more relevant to a particular activity.

Signing in

Obtain a signature from someone in the room who fits the following descriptor. Only one signature per person (even though one person may fit more than one descriptor).

Time allowed five minutes

- Plays sport:
- Enjoys gardening:
- Likes travelling:
- Reads books:
- Has children:
- Plays an instrument:
- Lived on abroad:
- Owns a pet:

- Speaks English:
- Your signature:

Tell me about yourself

In pairs (or threes) find out six really interesting things about your colleague. Topic suggestions may include e.g.

- Name
- Month of birthday
- Shoe size
- Place of birth
- Height
- Place of work
- Hobby
- Last holiday
- Pets
- Preferred sport
- Favourite colour
- Favourite food
- Favourite book
- First job
- Job title
- Personal achievement

Then introduce each other to the rest of the course revealing the six interesting facts, e.g. This is Zak he's an archivist, he has three children, his hobbies include playing the drums, last year in New Zealand he went white water rafting and is currently writing up his PhD thesis.

Alliterative assignations

Each person is to think of an adjective that describes him/herself. The word must be alliterative with the forename or preferred name e.g. Athletic Angela, Brainy Brian, Gorgeous Gussie, Naughty Nigel, Surfing Steven, Zany Zena.

Allowable exceptions – where the forename has alternative spellings or pronunciation sounds like another letter e.g. Canny Kate (Cate), Jolly Gemma (Jemma), Fabulous Philip, Irresistible Eileen.

Each person then introduces him/herself using the alliterative adjective, e.g. Hello I'm Happy Henrietta who are you? – Hello I'm Energetic Eddie.

The group can revisit the exercise during the course to see how many adjectives they can remember.

Huggy bears

Ask the participants to form groups according to a topic heading, e.g. find all the people born in the same month as yourself. Form groups by:

- Month of birth (e.g. January, February, March etc.)
- Favourite drink (e.g. tea, beer, water)
- Gender (e.g. male, female)
- Professional group (e.g. web designers, nurses, librarians)
- Pets (e.g. cat, dog, fish, zoo)
- Place of birth/country of birth
- Shoe size
- Football team
- Type of house or residence

- Favourite colour
- Number of children

Silent movement

The object of this exercise is to get the participants in a structured line but without speaking.

Ask the participants to form a line down the room, then without talking they must change positions to re-form the line according to a given topic heading. Indicate which way the line is to form, e.g. tallest this end shortest that end.

Without speaking form a line according to, e.g. by

- Height
- Place of birth (A–Z)
- Shoe size
- Year of birth
- Month of birth (January – December)

Check if participants have achieved the task

Circle the alphabet

The object of this exercise is to form an alphabetical circle according the forenames. Indicate where A will stand then clockwise round to Z (or Z to A).

Standing in a circle, ask the participants to introduce themselves to the colleagues on either side. After each introduction, the participants move (one place) in the direction that will form an alphabetical circle by forenames. Following each move, participants introduce themselves to the next colleague, and then move again until the circle is complete.

For example, present order of circle is: Tom – Margaret – Susan – Jane – Michael – Zachary – Ziba – Ania – Dezi. Required order of circle is: Ania – Dezi – Jane – Margaret – Michael – Susan – Tom – Zachary – Ziba (or Ziba – Zachary – Tom – Susan – Michael – Margaret – Jane – Dezi – Ania).

This can be repeated using with surnames, e.g. present order of circle is: Smith – Jones – Brown – Green – Black – Patel – Singh – Kerr – Ryan; required order is: Black – Brown – Green – Jones – Kerr – Patel – Ryan – Singh – Smith.

Appendix E
Chartered Institute of Library and Information Professionals code of ethics

The following text has been reproduced with permission of the Chartered Institute of Library and Information Professionals.

Ethical principles and code of professional practice for library and information professionals

Library and information professionals are frequently the essential link between information users and the information or piece of literature which they require. They therefore occupy a privileged position which carries corresponding responsibilities. In addition, whether they are self-employed or employed, their position is sometimes a sensitive one, which may impose a need to balance conflicting requirements.

The purpose of the Principles and Code which follow this introduction is to provide a framework to help library and information professionals, who are members of CILIP, to manage the responsibilities and sensitivities which figure prominently in their work. There is a statement of Ethical Principles and a more extended Code of Professional Practice, which applies these principles to the different groups and professionals to which our members must relate. The Code also makes some additional points with regard to professional behaviour. Given the diversity of the information profession, it is inevitable that not every statement in the Code of Professional Practice will be equally applicable to every member of CILIP. However, the Ethical Principles ought to command more general support, even though some members may not feel the force of each one of them to the same extent in their day-to-day experience. The Principles and Code assume that respect for duly enacted law is a fundamental responsibility for everybody.

By the terms of its Royal Charter, CILIP has a responsibility to "the public good". It is therefore anticipated that our Ethical Principles and our Code of Professional Practice may be of interest well beyond the immediate limits of the membership of CILIP, both to those whose work bears close comparison with ours, and also to those who may, from time to time, want a clear statement of our ethical principles and what we consider to be good professional practice.

Associated with these Principles and Code, there is a growing collection of practical examples, illustrating how information professionals and others can use the Principles and Code to help them cope with ethical dilemmas they may face. In further support of the Principles and Code, CILIP has established an Ethics Panel of experienced members of the profession, and they and the professional staff of CILIP are available to members who may need additional help in resolving ethical issues.

CILIP's Disciplinary Regulations provide that a Member will be guilty of professional misconduct if he/she has acted contrary to the aims, objects and interests of CILIP or in a manner unbecoming or prejudicial to the profession. In reaching decisions under the Disciplinary Procedure, regard will be had to the Statement of Ethical Principles and the Code of Professional Practice and Members should therefore be aware that failure to comply with the Principles and Code may, depending on the circumstances, be a ground for disciplinary action.

Ethical principles for library and information professionals

The conduct of members should be characterised by the following general principles, presented here in no particular order of priority:

1. Concern for the public good in all professional matters, including respect for diversity within society, and the promoting of equal opportunities and human rights.

2. Concern for the good reputation of the information profession.

3. Commitment to the defence, and the advancement, of access to information, ideas and works of the imagination.

4. Provision of the best possible service within available resources.

5. Concern for balancing the needs of actual and potential users and the reasonable demands of employers.

6. Equitable treatment of all information users.

7. Impartiality, and avoidance of inappropriate bias, in acquiring and evaluating information and in mediating it to other information users.

8. Respect for confidentiality and privacy in dealing with information users.

9. Concern for the conservation and preservation of our information heritage in all formats.

10. Respect for, and understanding of, the integrity of information items and for the intellectual effort of those who created them.

11. Commitment to maintaining and improving personal professional knowledge, skills and competences.

12. Respect for the skills and competences of all others, whether information professionals or information users, employers or colleagues.

Code of professional practice for library and information professionals

This Code applies the ethical principles to the different groups and interests to which CILIP members must relate. The Code also makes some additional points with regard to professional behaviour. The principles and values will differ in their relative importance according to context.

A: Personal responsibilities

People who work in the information profession have personal responsibilities which go beyond those immediately implied by their contract with their employers or clients. Members should therefore:

1. strive to attain the highest personal standard of professional knowledge and competence

2. ensure they are competent in those branches of professional practice in which qualifications and/or experience entitle them to engage by keeping abreast of developments in their areas of expertise

3. claim expertise in areas of library and information work or in other disciplines only where their skills and knowledge are adequate

B: Responsibilities to information and its users

The behaviour of professionals who work with information should be guided by a regard for the interests and needs of information users. People working in the information profession also need to be conscious that they have responsibility for a growing heritage of information and data, irrespective of format. This includes works of the imagination as well as factual data. Members should therefore:

1. ensure that information users are aware of the scope and remit of the service being provided

2. make the process of providing information, and the standards and procedures governing that process, as clear and open as possible

3. avoid inappropriate bias or value judgements in the provision of services

4. protect the confidentiality of all matters relating to information users, including their enquiries, any services to be provided, and any aspects of the users' personal circumstances or business

5. deal fairly with the competing needs of information users, and resolve conflicting priorities with due regard for the urgency and importance of the matters being considered

6. deal promptly and fairly with any complaints from information users, and keep them informed about progress in the handling of their complaints.

7. ensure that the information systems and services for which they are responsible are the most effective, within the resources available, in meeting the needs of users

8. ensure that the materials to which they provide access are those which are most appropriate to the needs of legitimate users of the service

9. defend the legitimate needs and interests of information users, while upholding the moral and legal rights of the creators and distributors of intellectual property

10. respect the integrity of information sources, and cite sources used, as appropriate

11. show an appropriate concern for the future information needs of society through the long-term preservation and conservation of materials as required, as well as an understanding of proper records management

C: Responsibilities to colleagues and the information community

The personal conduct of information professionals at work should promote the profession in the best possible manner at all times. Members should therefore:

1. act in ways that promote the profession positively, both to their colleagues and to the public at large

2. afford respect and understanding to other colleagues and professionals and acknowledge their ideas, contributions and work, wherever and whenever appropriate

3. refer to colleagues in a professional manner and not discredit or criticise their work unreasonably or inappropriately

4. when working in an independent capacity, conduct their business in a professional manner that respects the legitimate rights and interests of others

5. encourage colleagues, especially those for whom they have a line-management responsibility, to maintain and enhance their professional knowledge and competence

6. refrain from ascribing views to, or speaking on behalf of, CILIP, unless specifically authorised to do so

7. report significant breaches of this Code to the appropriate authorities

8. refrain from any behaviour in the course of their work which might bring the information profession into disrepute

D: Responsibilities to society

One of the distinguishing features of professions is that their knowledge and skills are at the service of society at large, and do not simply serve the interests of the immediate customer. Members should therefore:

1. consider the public good, both in general and as it refers to particular vulnerable groups, as well as the immediate claims arising from their employment and their professional duties

2. promote equitable access for all members of society to public domain information of all kinds and in all formats

3. strive to achieve an appropriate balance within the law between demands from information users, the need to respect confidentiality, the terms of their employment, the public good and the responsibilities outlined in this Code

4. encourage and promote wider knowledge and acceptance of, and wider compliance with, this Code, both among colleagues in the information professions and more widely among those whom we serve

Responsibilities as employees

Members who are employed have duties that go beyond the immediate terms of their employment contract. On occasion these may conflict with the immediate demands of their employer but be in the broader interest of the public and possibly the employer themselves. Members should therefore:

1. develop a knowledge and understanding of the organisation in which they work and use their skills and expertise to promote the legitimate aims and objectives of their employer

2. avoid engaging in unethical practices during their work and bring to the attention of their employer any concerns they may have concerning the ethics or legality of specific decisions, actions or behaviour at work

Updated: 03 February 2006

Registered charity no. 313014

© Copyright CILIP 2006

CILIP, 7 Ridgmount Street, London WC1E 7AE

Tel: +44 (0)20 7255 0500 Fax: +44 (0)20 7255 0501

Appendix F
Chartered Institute of Library and Information Professionals certification scheme handbook

The following text has been reproduced with permission of the Chartered Institute of Library and Information Professionals.

Contents

1 Introduction

Certification is a recognition of the contribution made in library and information work by para-professionals. Affiliated Members of CILIP may apply for Certification. You will either:

- have been working in library and information work for five years or more (full-time equivalent) [Category 1 applicants].

  or

- have been working in library and information work for two years (full-time equivalent) and have participated in work-based training or other staff development [Category 2 applicants].

(See Certification Regulation No.1).

Support in the certification process is available in all Branches and Home Nations of CILIP and assessment for this award is also carried out locally, except in the case of overseas members. The process involves the following steps. You are strongly advised to read ALL the guidelines before you begin, especially the criteria for assessment (Section 2).

1.1 Checklist

1. Make sure that you are a current Affiliated Member of CILIP.

2. Read the Certification Regulations (see Appendix 4.1).

3. Identify your Regional CPD Officer (see Section 3.2).

4. Make use of the support network provided by the Career Development Group (CDG) (see Section 3.2).

5. Attend a course organised by the Career Development Group (CDG) or the Affiliated Members National

Committee. Information about these courses may be found on the CILIP website, in Gazette or through your Regional CPD Officer. If you are unable to attend such a course please contact the Qualifications and Professional Development Department of CILIP for advice.

6. Complete your portfolio.

Category 1 candidates:

This must include your application form, CV, a personal statement demonstrating experience and/or experiential learning, a Personal Development Plan (PDP), and a supporting letter, which should evidence achievement and indicate potential for future development where appropriate. You may also include copies of relevant certificates or equivalents (see Section 2 criteria for assessment and Section 3.5 for further information).

Category 2 candidates:

This must include your application form, CV, a personal statement reflecting the outcomes of your learning, copies of certificates or equivalents, a PDP, and a supporting letter which should evidence achievement and indicate potential for future development where appropriate (see Section 2 a criteria for assessment and Section 3.5 for further information).

7. When you are ready to submit your application, contact the Qualifications and Professional Development Department. This will enable CILIP to verify your contact details and deal with any queries. The Department will confirm the appropriate address to which you should send your application.

Figure 1.2 Framework schema diagram

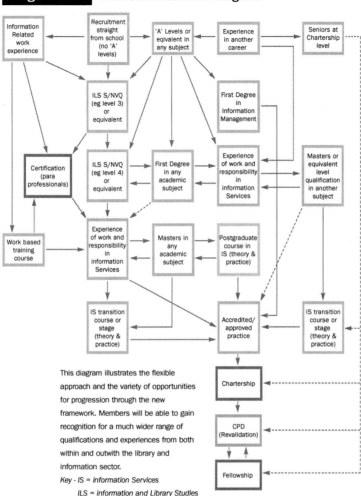

This diagram illustrates the flexible approach and the variety of opportunities for progression through the new framework. Members will be able to gain recognition for a much wider range of qualifications and experiences from both within and outwith the library and information sector.

Key - IS = Information Services
ILS = Information and Library Studies

8. Your application will be assessed by a local CILIP Assessment Panel (CAP) (see Section 3.7). You will be informed of the results by letter.

9. If your application is not successful you will receive copies of the assessments by all members of the panel, advice on reapplication and information on the

appeals procedure. You should contact your Regional CPD Officer for further information (see Section 3.8).

10. Consider progressing to Chartership (see Section 3.9)!

2 Certification assessment criteria

Certified Affiliates maintain and manage many aspects of library and information services. They may be responsible for practical or technical work and may also be involved in the management and development of staff and services.

To apply for certification all candidates must demonstrate:

1. an ability to evaluate personal performance and service performance (use the template)

2. an understanding of the importance of Continuing Professional Development (Personal Development Plan)

3. an appreciation of the role and contribution of library and information services in the wider community (use the template)

In addition

Category 1 candidates:

Candidates will be expected to demonstrate:

an appreciation of their personal technical and professional skills developed through practice (use the template).

Category 2 candidates:

Candidates will be expected to demonstrate:

an ability to evaluate training and development activities and to demonstrate a growing awareness of the relationship between theory and practice (use the template).

3 Guidelines

3.1 Membership of CILIP

All applicants must be in current membership of CILIP. To join as an Affiliated Member contact CILIP at: *www.cilip.org.uk/membership/categories.*

3.2 Regional support

3.2.1 Regional CPD officers

The Home Nations and Regional Branches of CILIP have a named officer to provide information on the Certification process and to deal with queries. They can advise you on the correct category of application and help you to find a mentor if appropriate. A list of these officers is available on the CILIP website at: *www.cilip.org.uk/qualificationschartership.*

3.2.2 Support network

There is also a support network, currently operated by the Career Development Group (CDG), whose members provide advice and guidance to candidates working towards Certification. For details of your nearest support network member please check the CDG website at: *www.career developmentgroup.org.uk.*

The supporter can advise you on collecting evidence for your portfolio and how to use that evidence to meet the criteria for assessment. They will also advise you on your PDP. They may also be able to suggest appropriate training or self-development activities.

3.2.3 Support for applicants living or working outside the UK

Members living and/or working outside the UK should initially contact the Qualifications and Professional Development Department at CILIP (Email: *quals@cilip.org.uk*).

3.3 Mentoring scheme

You are strongly advised to work with a mentor whilst preparing for certification. Many organisations already have a mentoring scheme or equivalent in operation and CILIP advise that where appropriate you make use of that scheme. However, CILIP also has a Mentor Scheme whose members are mainly based in the Home Nations and Regions. There are some mentors who work outside the UK.

You can find a suitable mentor by using the Mentor database held on the CILIP website: *www.cilip.org.uk/ qualificationschartership* or by contacting your Regional CPD Officer or the Qualifications and Professional Development Department at CILIP (Email: *quals@cilip .org.uk*). For overseas members CILIP may suggest a virtual mentor where appropriate.

All mentors receive training in supporting candidates and can provide very useful help and advice (information on mentor training is available at *www.cilip.org.uk/ qualificationschartership*).

3.4 Training events

The Career Development Group (www.careerdevelop mentgroup.org.uk) and the Affiliated Members National Committee (*www.cilip.org.uk/groups/amnc/amnc.html*) organise specific training events in all CILIP Regions and the

Home Nations. At these events you can get guidance on completion of the templates, PDPs, applications and mentoring. It is also a good opportunity to meet other certification candidates. Other very valuable training events to support your application are offered by all specialist groups within CILIP.

If you are unable to attend a training event for Certification please contact the Qualifications and Professional Development Department at CILIP for advice (Email: *quals@cilip.org.uk*).

3.5 Portfolio preparation

NB All documents, other than the application form must be word processed and the font should be a minimum of 12-point type size.

3.5.1 Application form

A copy of the form can be downloaded from the CILIP website: *www.cilip.org.uk/qualificationschartership* or obtained from the Qualifications and Professional Development Department (Email: *quals@cilip.org.uk*).

3.5.2 Curriculum Vitae (CV)

Your CV should detail your work experience, educational qualifications and training activities; the information should be given in reverse date order, i.e. most recent experience/ qualifications first. It should also include any relevant experience outside work e.g. professional activities, committee or voluntary work.

3.5.3 Personal statement

Please download and complete a copy of the appropriate template at: *www.cilip.org.uk/qualificationschartership*. The personal statement, including the summary (maximum of 500 words), should be no longer than 4 × A4 sheets and should only be on one side of the paper.

Examples of anonymised personal statements can be found at: *www.cilip.org.uk/qualificationschartership*.

Category 1 applicants:

You need to reflect on your work experience and comment on what skills and expertise you have learned under each of the headings provided on the template. You also need to provide a summary of your personal development in the workplace. You should also take the opportunity to reflect on any training you have received; how it has affected your knowledge and understanding and the way you work. Avoid description and focus on a critical analysis of your performance.

Category 2 applicants:

You need to reflect on the training you have received; how that training has affected your work, and if appropriate the work of the organisation. You also need to provide a summary of how your practical knowledge and understanding have been developed through the training activities. You may include a wide range of training and other development activities. Advice on activities to include can be provided by your Mentor, or the appropriate member of the support network. Information on additional training and development activities will also be available on the CILIP website: *www.cilip.org.uk/training*.

Certificates of training or equivalent should be sent with your application. If you are submitting an electronic application, copies of the certificates can be sent separately accompanied by a copy of your application form.

3.5.4 Personal development plan

You should provide a short statement on your plans to further your personal development. This statement should be no longer than 1 × A4 sheet and should be discussed with your Mentor and/or line manager before application. Your PDP should be realistic and have specific goals and outcomes. If you wish to progress to Chartered membership after gaining Certification you will be required to review and revise your PDP.

You may find it helpful to use the CILIP Body of Professional Knowledge (BPK) to audit your knowledge and skills and to identify areas for future development (this can be found on the CILIP website: *www.cilip.org.uk/qualificationschartership*). The BPK sets out the specialist knowledge that underpins all library and information work. You are not expected to be familiar with all the areas nor to have in-depth knowledge of a specific area, unless it is a particular requirement of your job. A matrix of skills and competencies appropriate for Certification is also on the website.

You may wish to attach copies of your staff appraisal or staff development and training record to support your plan. These will be treated in strict confidence.

Examples of anonymised personal development plans can be found at: *www.cilip.org.uk/qualificationschartership*.

3.5.5 Supporting letter

Normally this letter should be written by a Chartered Member of CILIP. Specific attention should be given to your achievements and should indicate potential for agreed future development. If your line manager or Mentor is not a Chartered Member of CILIP they can still be asked to provide the letter if they are the person who can best endorse your application and your suitability for Certification.

Guidelines for the supporting letter can be found on the CILIP website: *www.cilip.org.uk/qualificationschartership.*

3.6 Application

When you have assembled all the elements of your portfolio it is a good idea to show it to your Mentor or a member of the regional support network.When you are ready to submit your application, contact the Qualifications and Professional Development Department (Email: *quals@cilip.org.uk*). This will enable CILIP to verify your contact details and deal with any queries. The Department will confirm the appropriate address to which you should send your application.

The Qualifications and Professional Development Department will also advise you of the timetable for the submission of applications to the CILIP Assessment Panels (See Section 3.7.2). This information is also available on the CILIP website: *www.cilip.org.uk/qualificationschartership.* Normally, applications must be received by the last working day in any quarter-year for assessment to be completed within the following quarter.

Send two copies of your portfolio (in printed format or on disk/CD) to the contact address. Remember to keep a copy for yourself.

You may submit your application as a web page if you prefer. (If you are sending an electronic submission but also wish to send copies of printed material as evidence, please attach a copy of the original application form with the printed material, and enclose a stamped addressed envelope).

All candidates who submit in printed format or by disk/CD must also enclose a stamped addressed envelope for receipt. Electronic applications will be acknowledged electronically.

If you are including in your evidence reference to words, ideas, structure or data by others, remember it is essential to acknowledge their contribution, through complete, accurate and specific citation.

3.7 Assessment

3.7.1 Procedure

On receipt your application will be processed and sent to two members of the CILIP Assessment Panel (See Section 3.7.2). If there is a disagreement between the panel members, a third panel member, normally a member of CILIP Chartership Board, will be asked to look at the documents. Your application will not be assessed by anyone who works for the same organisation as you. All material will be treated in a confidential manner.

If your application does not adequately meet the criteria you may be asked to provide additional written information or documentary evidence or you may be asked to attend an informal interview. If your application is unsuccessful you will be able to reapply. You will be given a suggested resubmission date, together with feedback (see Section 3.7.4).

3.7.2 CILIP assessment panels

All applications are assessed by members of the CAPs in CILIP Regional Branches/Home Nations. Members of CAPs are drawn from a wide variety of backgrounds and have experience gained in a range of information and library work. They are all trained in assessment and many of them may also be assessors for other qualifications. For details of the Terms of Reference of the Panels please see the CILIP website: *www.cilip.org.uk/aboutcilip*.

3.7.3 Notification

Normally you will receive an acknowledgement, within 10 working days, that your application has been received.

Your Regional CPD Officer will notify the Regional Branch/Home Nation and the Qualifications and Professional Development Department of the results of all applications. Qualifications and Professional Development Department will inform the Chartership Board. All successful applicants will receive a letter confirming their results, together with a Certificate.

Once you have received notification of being successful you are entitled to use the post-nominal letters ACLIP. If you have any queries please contact your Regional CPD Officer or the Qualifications and Professional Development Department (Email: *quals@cilip.org.uk*).

3.7.4 Feedback

All candidates whose initial application cannot be immediately accepted will receive feedback from the Panel. This will take the form of copies of all assessment sheets completed by the Panel. The comments are intended to help you review your portfolio and to provide guidance to assist you in re-application. Panel members who were involved in the original assessment will not assess subsequent reapplications.

3.8 Appeals

If your application is unsuccessful you may appeal, according to procedures approved by Council. A copy of the Appeals Procedures will be sent to unsuccessful candidates. (See Appendix 4.2).

3.9 Progression to Chartership

After becoming an ACLIP you may decide that you would like to progress to being a Chartered Member of CILIP. You should talk to your regional supporter or your Mentor, who will be able to help you plan your way forward. You will also need a Chartership Handbook, available at: *www.cilip.org.uk/qualificationschartership*.

After receiving your ACLIP you will normally be expected to work for two years (full-time equivalent) before submitting an application for Chartered Membership. During that time you can register as a Chartership candidate but you will have to become an Associate Member before you can submit your Chartership portfolio. This may mean a change in your subscription rate. Personal advice will be provided by the Qualifications and Professional Development Department or the Regional Support Network after you have become an ACLIP.

You will need to meet the criteria for Chartered Member status, so it is important that you understand those requirements before you register as a candidate. You, and your Mentor, will need to plan your Personal Professional Development Plan carefully, based on your own situation. You will be expected to review and revise your Certification PDP to provide a structured framework for your training and development during this period.

Many large organisations will have a training scheme in place, which will help you to gain additional knowledge and understanding of the principles of professional membership. Advice can always be obtained from the Qualifications and Professional Development Department (Email: *quals@ cilip.org.uk*).

Information on formal education courses and other training activities that will help you plan your own programme of personal development will be available on the CILIP website: *www.cilip.org.uk/training*.

4 Appendices

4.1 Regulations (2005 Regulations drawn up under Byelaw 11)

1. Registration

    All applicants must be current members of CILIP (Affiliated Member or Associate Member).

    There are two categories of application:

    Category 1: all applicants must be members currently employed in library and information work who have worked for five or more years full-time equivalent.

    NB No further applications under Category 1 will be accepted after 31st December 2008

    Category 2: all applicants must be members currently employed in library and information work for two or more years, who have either:

    taken part in work-based learning activities within their own organisation

    or

have been involved in relevant out of work self-development activities.

Registration forms are available via the CILIP website at *www.cilip.org.uk/qualificationschartership* or in the CILIP Handbook for Certification.

If you are unsure which category you fall into please contact the CILIP Qualifications and Professional Development Department for advice and guidance (*quals@cilip.org.uk*).

2 Application

2.1 Category 1 applicants

Each applicant will submit a portfolio including: Application form

Curriculum Vitae

Personal statement, of no more than 4 × A4 sheets, demonstrating experience and/or experiential learning against agreed criteria.

A personal development plan

A supporting letter which should evidence achievement and indicate potential for future development, where appropriate (CILIP will supply a template for this purpose).

2.2 Category 2 applicants

Each applicant will submit a portfolio including:

Application form

Curriculum Vitae

A personal statement, of no more than 4 × A4 sheets, reflecting on the outcomes of their certificated learning and their experience, against agreed criteria.

Copies of certificates or equivalent relating to training

A Personal Development Plan

A supporting letter which should evidence achievement and indicate potential for future development, where appropriate (CILIP will supply a template for this purpose).

2.3 Notes on submission

All applications must be in the English or Welsh language

The CV and supporting letter should be word-processed

The application form, personal statement, and Personal Development Plan should be on the designated form

Electronic submission is acceptable, but copies of certificates etc. may be sent by post accompanied by a copy of your application form

All applications for assessment should be accompanied by the appropriate fee, to be determined annually by CILIP AGM

Confidentiality

All applications (electronic and hard copy) will be stored and treated in a confidential manner by CILIP Assessment Panels.

3 Assessment

Each application will normally be assessed by CILIP Assessment Panels in the Member's Branch or Home Nation. The submission should be sent to the named Officer of the CILIP Regional Branch or Home Nation. A full list of these officers is available on the website at *www.cilip.org.uk/qualificationschartership/* or from the Qualifications and Professional Development Department.

Overseas members should submit their applications to the Qualifications and Professional Development Department in the first instance.

All applicants will be notified of the outcome in writing within 10 working days of the date of the assessment meeting. All documents will be returned to successful applicants once Certification has been confirmed.

3.1 Criteria for assessment

All applicants will have gained knowledge and experience of library and information work in a variety of roles and should be able to reflect on that experience, using the templates provided.

All candidates must demonstrate:

1. an ability to evaluate personal performance and service performance

2. an understanding of the importance of Continuing Professional Development.

3. an appreciation of the role and contribution of library and information services in the wider community.

In addition

Category 1 candidates:

Candidates will be expected to demonstrate:

an appreciation of their personal technical and professional skills developed through practice

Category 2 candidates:

Candidates will be expected to demonstrate:

an ability to evaluate training and development activities and to demonstrate a growing awareness of the relationship between theory and practice.

3.2 Form of assessment

The CILIP Assessment Panel will determine a method for the additional assessment of any application, if necessary, which may include either of the following:

(a) a request for additional written information or documentary evidence

(b) a request for the candidate to attend an interview

3.3 Admission to the Certification Register

The date of admission to the register will normally be that on which the CILIP Assessment Panel accepts the application.

Once admitted to the Register you must remain in membership of CILIP to retain the use of the post nominal letters ACLIP and to describe yourself as a Certified Member.

4 Appeals

Candidates whose applications are rejected have a right of Appeal, according to procedures approved by Council. A copy of the Appeals Procedures will be sent to unsuccessful candidates (see Appendix 4.1.1 to these Regulations).

5 Progression to Chartership

ACLIPs will be eligible to apply for Chartered Membership. Information on applying for Chartership can be found at *www.cilip.org.uk/qualifications-chartership* or from the Qualifications and Professional Development Department.

In order to progress to Chartered Membership you must be an Associate Member.

4.2 Appeals procedure

1. An appeal may be made against a decision of the Assessment Panel not to accept a candidate's Application for Certification.

2. A candidate whose submission is not accepted will be sent the following documents by Recorded Delivery:

(a) A letter informing the candidate of the decision and the date of the Assessment Panel meeting at which it was made.

(b) A summary of the points made at the Assessment Panel meeting and copies of the assessment documents of Panel members, setting out the reasons for rejection.

(c) A copy of this Appeals Procedure.

3. A candidate who wishes to appeal against the decision of the Assessment Panel must do so within six weeks of the date of receipt of the Recorded Delivery letter referred to in 2. The Appeal must be made in writing to the Chief Executive.

4. The only grounds on which an Appeal may be made are:

(a) That all or part of the information used by the Assessment Panel was biased or incorrect due to no fault of the candidate and that the Panel did not know this at the time it took its decision.

(b) That the Assessment Panel failed to follow its own published procedures and that this materially affected its decision.

5. The Chief Executive will decide whether there is a prima facie case for appeal. Where there is not s/he will inform the candidate of the reason for his/her ruling. In such cases there will be no further appeal.

6. Where there is a prima facie case for appeal the Chief Executive will select an Appeal Panel of three from a panel chosen annually by Council from amongst its membership for this purpose. (These may not be members of a CILIP Assessment Panel, or the Chartership Board).

7. The Chief Executive will set a date for the hearing of the Appeal to take place within six weeks of the date of receipt of the candidate's written Appeal.

8. The Chief Executive will send to each member appointed to the Appeal Panel a copy of the candidate's portfolio submission, the papers sent to the candidate referred to in 2 above, and any papers sent by the candidate in support of his/her Appeal.

9. The candidate will be invited to attend the hearing of the Appeal and may be accompanied by a supporter. A representative of the CILIP Assessment Panel and the Head, Qualifications and Professional Development Department (or the nominee of either) should be present to represent the Assessment Panel and its office based procedures.

10. At an Appeal Panel hearing the matters for consideration will be limited to:

(a) Evidence from the candidate concerning the grounds for the Appeal, and details of how the information and/or procedures were faulty. The candidate should offer the correct information to the Appeal Panel. Panel members may question both the candidate and the representative of the Assessment Panel. The Assessment Panel representative should explain the reasons for any failure to comply with published procedures.

(b) The candidate may ask the supporter to speak on matters concerning the grounds for the Appeal. The supporter may not assist (or speak for) the appellant in answering professional questions put by the Panel.

(c) The Appeal Panel will be concerned solely to test the candidate's claim that the Assessment Panel used faulty information, biased statements or failed in its own procedures.

11. Where the Appeal Panel finds that the candidate's claim as set out in 10(c) has not been substantiated the Appeal must fail since the Assessment Panel may not be challenged on other grounds.

12. Where the Appeal Panel finds that the candidate has made the case they will instruct the Assessment Panel to review the matter. The Appeal Panel will give precise instructions to the Assessment Panel as to the evidence which must be considered, and what must be discounted. The Chair of the Appeal Panel will detail the evidence accepted by the Panel.The evidence and decision cannot be challenged by the Assessment Panel.

13. The Assessment Panel will review the case at its next meeting after the Appeal Panel hearing. The Panel will give written details of its decision to the Chief Executive and the Chair of the Professional Development Committee.

14. The Chief Executive will inform the candidate of the final decision of the Assessment Panel.

15. All candidates are eligible to reapply. No candidate will have to wait longer than one year to reapply for certification from the date of the original Panel decision.

4.3 Case studies

A joined the public library service in 1981, as full time library assistant. General library duties included issue, discharge of stock, dealing with the public, helping readers with requests. A worked in various branch libraries for 2 years and then worked in the Institute of Further and Higher Education College library for 2 years – general library duties, dealing with staff and pupils, ordering stock and cataloguing it, arranging staff timetables and periodical management in the library. Promoted to Senior Library Assistant with supervision of two Library Assistants.

S/he has now worked as Senior Library Assistant in the School of Music library for 3 years – ordering stock and catalogued music, music books, musical scores, sheet music for the various instruments, orchestra and bands, records, and maintained an up to date catalogue for staff and pupils to access. S/he has also prepared the sheet music for the youth orchestra, the youth chorale and the youth brass band associated with the school.

S/he has 7 'O' levels and 2 'A' levels.

A *could register interest in certification immediately and prepare a portfolio for application as a category 1 applicant in April 2005.*

B works for a small local authority in the Records Management Unit. S/he has worked there for 7 years and has recently has been given responsibility for assisting with Freedom of Information implementation. S/he helps with the awareness-raising presentations and preparing guidance on dealing with requests for information and gives advice on individual cases.

S/he has 4 O levels and 1 A level.

B *would apply for ACLIP in category 1*

C works in a large hospital and came directly from school with 2 A levels 2 years ago. S/he supports the Data Protection Officer on giving internal advice about the DP Act and helps to deal with requests from the public to see their own personal information. S/he has attended three external courses on Data Protection and has recently completed an ECDL course.

C *could apply for ACLIP in category 2*

D has worked in a University for over 12 years in various Support Services administrative posts but for the last two years has been focussing on Freedom of Information. S/he has a degree in Sociology and is now an Information Officer grade. To help in her current post, she has attended several external training events. S/he does not want to undertake further academic study.

D *could join CILIP and apply for ACLIP in Category 2 before trying for chartership.*

Appendix G
Chartered Institute of Library and Information Professionals chartered membership handbook

The following text has been reproduced with permission of the Chartered Institute of Library and Information Professionals.

Contents

1 Introduction

CILIP is committed to the development, maintenance and promotion of the highest levels of professional practice. Chartered Membership is the second level of professional qualification awarded by CILIP and is considered the 'gold standard' for information and library professionals. It is recognised throughout the world. The Institute recognises the dynamic nature of the information environment and the necessity to offer flexible routes for those wishing to gain recognition of their professional practice in information and library work. Chartered Membership is not an academic qualification but a recognition of the highest standards of professional practice and a commitment to undertake continuing professional development.

This Handbook will guide you through the steps you need to follow to achieve Chartered Membership status.

1.1 Checklist

Becoming a Chartered Member of CILIP involves the following steps. You are strongly advised to read ALL guidelines, especially the criteria for assessment, before you begin.

1. When you apply for Chartered Membership you must be a current Associate Member.

2. Complete and submit the Registration Form. With this form you must include:

    (i) Evidence of your educational qualification or CILIP Certification (original documents or certified copies). For details of recognised qualifications see the CILIP website: *www.cilip.org.uk/qualificationschartership*

(If your educational qualifications are not listed on the web site please contact Qualifications and Professional Development Department for advice in the first instance).

(ii) A Personal Professional Development Plan (PPDP). For details of required content see Section 3.1.2.

3. Register for the CILIP Mentor Scheme or undertake to participate in another approved mentor programme (see Section 3.1.4).

4. Complete the appropriate period of professional experience. For details of the period required see Section 3.2. During this period you should gather evidence for the portfolio that you will be required to submit to CILIP when you apply to become a Chartered Member. You should also meet regularly with your Mentor. Guidance on the structure and the contents of the portfolio are in Section 3.4.1.

5. Attend an approved advisory course, such as those organised by the Career Development Group (CDG). Information about these courses may be found on the CILIP website, in Gazette or through your local Support Network. If you are unable to attend such a course please contact the Qualifications and Professional Department of CILIP to arrange an alternative. You are advised to attend this course early in your period of professional experience, as it will help you with your application.

6. Inform the Qualifications and Professional Development Department when you have completed your required professional experience (see Section 3.4.2). You will normally be required to make your application for Chartered Membership within 1 year of

completing your required period of professional experience. In exceptional circumstances an extension to this period may be given. You must contact the Qualifications and Professional Department to request an extension before the original period expires.

7. Complete your portfolio. This must include:

   - an evaluative statement (maximum 1000 words) addressing the assessment criteria

   - the evidence

   - your Personal Professional Development Plan, with an analysis of the impact and effectiveness of your training

   - evidence of participation in the Mentor Scheme e.g. evidence of professional discussion

   See Section 2 for the Chartership assessment criteria and Section 3.4 for further information on your portfolio.

8. When you are ready to submit your portfolio, contact the Qualifications and Professional Development Department to request an application form. This will enable CILIP to verify contact details and deal with any queries.

9. Your portfolio will be assessed by the Chartership Board (see Section 3.5.1). Final decisions to accept or refer applications are taken by the Board at its regular meetings. Meeting dates and the schedule for sending in applications can be found on the CILIP website. You will be informed of the result immediately afterwards.

10. If your application is not initially successful you will be given feedback and/or clear guidance as to how you should proceed, together with a revised schedule (see Section 3.5.3).

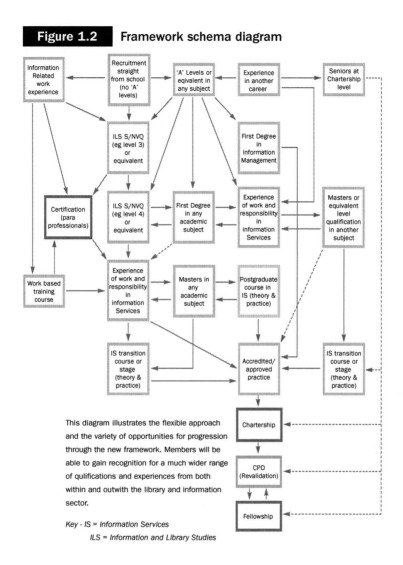

Figure 1.2 Framework schema diagram

This diagram illustrates the flexible approach and the variety of opportunities for progression through the new framework. Members will be able to gain recognition for a much wider range of qulifications and experiences from both within and outwith the library and information sector.

Key - IS = Information Services

ILS = Information and Library Studies

2 Criteria of assessment

All applications will be assessed against the same criteria. Candidates must demonstrate all of the following:

■ An ability to reflect critically on personal performance and to evaluate service performance

- Active commitment to continuing professional development
- An ability to analyse personal and professional development and progression with reference to experiential and developmental activities
- Breadth of professional knowledge and understanding of the wider professional context

Your application for Chartered Membership will take the form of a portfolio which shows evidence of your professional development since qualification, or since certification.

Your portfolio should address the assessment criteria and must include the following:

- a contents table
- your Curriculum Vitae (CV), including title and job descriptions of the posts you have held
- your completed Personal Professional Development Plan (PPDP)
- a personal evaluative statement (maximum 1000 words) which
    (i) explains why you chose the material included in your portfolio (links to assessment criteria)
    (ii) includes outcomes of developmental activities in which you have participated and an evaluation of how they have contributed to your professional development
    (iii) is cross referenced to other items in your portfolio
- Materials selected to show that you understand the objectives of the organisation and information

service/products and are able to analyse how effectively these objectives are met

- Organisational structure charts, where appropriate
- Evidence of participation in a mentor scheme

3 Guidelines

3.1 Registration

Under the terms of the Royal Charter awarded in 2002 the Chartered Institute of Library and Information Professionals maintains a professional Register of Chartered Members. To apply for Chartered Membership you should have been a member of CILIP for a minimum of one year and be in current membership when you submit your application for assessment. You must be a current Associate Member to apply (for further information see *www.cilip.org.uk/ membership/categories*).

There are two pathways to gain admittance to the Register (see 3.1.1 below). If you are unclear which pathway you need to follow you can contact the Qualifications and Professional Department at CILIP (Email: *quals@cilip .org.uk*) or your Regional CPD Officer, a list of whom can be found on the CILIP website: *www.cilip.org.uk/ qualificationschartership*

Complete a registration form available on the CILIP website at: *www.cilip.org.uk/qualificationschartership* and send it to CILIP with a copy of your PPDP and documentary evidence of your qualifications. You must also register for the CILIP Mentor Scheme or participate in another approved mentor scheme (see Section 3.1.4).

3.1.1 Pathways

You must have acceptable qualifications to be considered for Chartered Membership. You will either have:

- Pathway 1: a Library and Information Studies qualification recognised or accredited by CILIP at Scottish Qualifications Framework Level 10 or England Wales and Northern Ireland Framework Level HE4 (or above).

  OR you may have

- Pathway 2: CILIP Certification (ACLIP) plus evidence of a minimum period of further personal professional development (see Section 3.2.1).

  OR

- A recognised qualification listed on the CILIP website at: *www.cilip.org.uk/qualificationschartership*.

Applicants who obtained their qualifications outside the UK must provide evidence of their qualifications and of the appropriate period of professional experience before being accepted as candidates. Further advice is available from the Qualifications and Professional Development Department at CILIP (Email: *quals@cilip.org.uk*).

NB Candidates on both pathways must meet the same criteria of assessment for Chartership. (See Section 2)

3.1.2 Personal Professional Development Plan (PPDP)

This document (see the CILIP website for a template: *www.cilip.org.uk/qualificationschartership*) shows how you intend to ensure that your training and development activities, together with your professional experiences will help you to meet the assessment criteria. It will include:

- consideration of short and medium term development needs and how they will be met

- details of how you will achieve the goals you have set for yourself in order to meet the chartership assessment criteria (see Section 2)

- notes of who will support you e.g. mentors, employers, colleagues etc.

The PPDP should normally be countersigned by your Mentor.

Your Mentor and/or the Regional Support Network (see Section 3.3) will give you more advice on this. You may find the CILIP Body of Professional Knowledge available on the CILIP website at: *www.cilip.org.uk/ qualificationschartership* helpful in mapping your development needs. You should also be planning how to develop your skills and knowledge across the Body of Professional Knowledge in order to demonstrate your achievements against the assessment criteria (see Section 3.1.3). You can get further advice from the Qualifications and Professional Development Department at CILIP (Email: *quals@cilip.org.uk*).

3.1.3 Body of Professional Knowledge

The Body of Professional Knowledge (BPK), provides a useful reference tool to help you audit your current knowledge and skills and to identify areas that you may need to develop during your period of professional practice. The identification of areas for development will help you to prepare your PPDP and should also help you to evaluate your own performance against the PPDP in your portfolio.

3.1.4 Mentor Scheme

You are required to register with a Mentor, either through the CILIP Mentor Scheme or through another recognised mentoring scheme. If you are unsure whether a particular scheme is recognised please contact the Qualifications and Professional Development Department for advice. Information on the Mentor Scheme can be found on the CILIP website: *www.cilip.org.uk/qualificationschartership*.

Your Mentor will normally be a Chartered Member of CILIP and will have taken part in the mentoring training programme organised by CILIP. They will support you throughout the preparation period; giving advice on registration, training and development, gathering evidence for your portfolio, and enabling you to talk through issues and concerns in a non-threatening atmosphere. Normally, your Mentor will not be your line manager and, in some cases, not even from the same organisation.

You should keep a log or record of your meetings with your Mentor; these will provide evidence to enclose with your portfolio.

For applicants who both live and work outside the UK, CILIP may suggest a virtual mentor where appropriate.

3.2 Preparation period

3.2.1 Professional experience

Before you can submit your application for Chartered Membership you must have completed a minimum period of appropriate professional work experience. Normally, this will be in a designated professional post. However, it is the professional content of the job that matters and how it will help you to meet the criteria for assessment, rather than simply the job title. If you require advice on the level of appropriate professional experience please contact the Qualifications and Professional Development Department (Email: *quals@cilip.org.uk*).

Pathway 1: One year full-time equivalent (FTE) work in a library and information service or related environment.

Pathway 2: Two years (FTE) in a library and information service or related environment.

CILIP may authorise a reduction in the case of individual candidates who can demonstrate substantial relevant practical experience, which could have been gained in another discipline.

NB Full-time work is deemed to be not less than 30 hours per week. Advice on specific individual situations will be provided by the Qualifications and Professional Development Department: (Email: *quals@cilip.org.uk*).

3.2.2 Preparing your portfolio

When you apply for Chartered Membership you will do so by submitting a portfolio (see Section 3.4.1) so you need to plan this from the beginning of your preparation period. Your Mentor can advise you about this and you can get further information and support from the Regional Support Network and from the CILIP website: www.cilip.org.uk/ qualificationschartership, and from courses run by CILIP. You need to keep a record of your training and development activities and attend courses, such as those organised by the CILIP Career Development Group (CDG), CILIP Regional Branches and CILIP Special Interest Groups, and other professional networks.

3.2.3 Gathering evidence

You must keep copies of any certificates (or equivalent) for training courses you attend. You should also keep copies of any appraisal documents, presentations you have given, papers you have written, or any other documentary evidence of your professional activities. As well as keeping this evidence, you should try to get into the habit of reflecting on what you learned from these training and development activities and how they have impacted on your professional practice. You will be asked to reflect on your learning outcomes in your application so establish good practice from the beginning!

Remember that all materials in your portfolio should be there because they demonstrate achievement against one or more of the assessment criteria.

A number of titles and other sources of practical information on portfolio building and reflective practice can be found on the CILIP website: *www.cilip.org.uk/qualificationschartership*.

You should start collecting material for inclusion in your portfolio as soon as you qualify or obtain your certification, as it is more difficult to gather documents etc. after a period of time has elapsed, particularly if you have changed jobs in the meantime. You may not need all the material that you gather but it is important that you gather a wide range of materials from which you can select evidence.

3.3 Support

There is a variety of support for you as you work towards Chartership.

3.3.1 Regional CPD officer

The Home Nations and Regional Branches of CILIP have a named officer to provide information for Members on qualifications. A list of these officers is available on the CILIP website at: *www.cilip.org.uk/ qualificationschartership*.

3.3.2 Your Mentor

It is important that you keep in regular contact with your Mentor and discuss your practical experience, development and training issues and preparation of your portfolio. All CILIP Mentors receive training in supporting candidates and can provide very useful support and advice. Information on mentor training can be found at *www.cilip.org/ qualificationschartership*. If your Mentor is not a Member, you can get additional information from the Regional CPD Officer (see Section 3.3.1) or the Support Network in your own area (see Section 3.3.3).

3.3.3 Support Network

There is a Support Network, currently operated by the Career Development Group (CDG), whose members provide advice and guidance to candidates working towards Chartership. For details of your nearest support network contact please check the CDG website: *www.careerdevelopmentgroup.org.uk*.

Your local support network member can advise you on collecting evidence for your portfolio and how to use that evidence to meet the criteria for assessment. They will also advise you on your PPDP. They may also be able to suggest appropriate training or self-development activities. Often they will also be involved in running the courses which help you to prepare your portfolio (see Sections 3.2.2 and 3.4). They are experienced Chartered Members who themselves receive training and support from CILIP, and quite often they will have experience of assessment of professional qualifications.

3.3.4 Employer support

The significant relationship for any candidate will be that between themselves and their Mentor, which places the principle emphasis on a process of self-directed learning to take account of variety of specialist needs within rapidly changing range of environments.

The support of employers is also very important to individual candidates who will benefit from a structured internal training programme that takes into account the objectives of the particular library environment in which they work as well as the wider world of professional practice. CILIP welcomes reference in job advertisements from employers who conform to CILIP guidelines for good practice, for example through the provision of a mentoring scheme.

Employers can also have a key role to play supporting candidates in a number of practical ways, for example by encouraging them to attend appropriate professional meetings that may occur during normal work time or by offering a short study break for completion of an application for Chartered Membership. An employers information pack containing advice and guidance for employers who wish to support the qualifications process can be found on the CILIP website: *www.cilip.org/qualificationschartership*.

3.3.5 Chartership application advisory course

CILIP Career Development Group run courses, in all Regional Branches and Home Nations, specifically for Members seeking Chartered Member status. At these courses you will meet other candidates and you will be able to talk through the whole process. You are strongly advised to attend this course early in your period of practical experience, as it will help you organise your time and prepare your portfolio. These courses are listed in Gazette and on the CDG website: *www.careerdevelopmentgroup.org.uk.*

If you are unable to attend a Chartership application advisory course please contact the Qualifications and Professional Development Department for advice (Email: *quals@cilip.org.uk*).

3.3.6 Other courses

In addition there are many courses run by CILIP, the Regional Branches and other CILIP Specialist Interest Groups, as well as other training providers, that you may find extremely helpful in preparing your portfolio and meeting your own development needs. Contact your Regional CPD officer for more information or look at the CILIP website: *www.cilip.org.uk/qualificationscharterrship.*

3.3.7 Members living and working outside the UK

CILIP welcomes applications for Chartered Membership from applicants who live and work outside the UK. Advice to these members will be provided initially by the Qualifications and Professional Development Department with further support both through the Mentor Scheme and through the support network.

3.3.8 lis-cilip-reg

You should also consider joining this discussion list. The list provides a forum for discussing practical issues concerned with chartering as well as an opportunity to discuss topical issues of current concern within the profession. Information professionals in all sectors are welcome to contribute to the list.

To join the list, send the command:

Join lis-cilip-reg "forename" "family name" (all in one line and in the main body of the text, not the subject field) to the JISCmail SERVER at *Jiscmail@jiscmail.ac.uk*.

Follow the instructions that will be mailed to you as soon as your message is accepted by JiscMail.

3.4 Application

Once you have completed your period of practical experience, you should inform the Qualifications and Professional Development Department. You are expected to submit your portfolio within one year of completing the period of professional experience. If you need to apply for an extension to this period you must do so before the date you have been given for completion.

Your application for Chartered Membership will take the form of a portfolio which shows evidence of your professional development since qualification, or since certification.

3.4.1 Portfolio

Your portfolio must include the following:

- a contents table
- your Curriculum Vitae (CV), including title and job descriptions of the posts you have held
- your completed Personal Professional Development Plan (PPDP)
- a personal and evaluative statement (maximum 1000 words) which:
  - (i) explains why you chose the material included in your portfolio (links to assessment criteria)

(ii) includes outcomes of developmental activities in which you have participated and an evaluation of how they have contributed to your professional development

(iii) is cross referenced to other items in your portfolio

- materials selected to show that you understand the objectives of the organisation and information service/products and are able to analyse how effectively these objectives are met

- organisational structure charts, where appropriate

- evidence of participation in a mentor scheme

All candidates do not have the same level of direct experience. However you are expected to demonstrate the steps you have taken to make up for a lack of practical experience. This may be through training and development activities, attendance at meetings, research, involvement in professional networks, both real and virtual. Your Mentor, or appropriate member of the Regional Support Network will give advice on this.

You will be demonstrating your professional judgment in the selection and organisation of your evidence. The emphasis is on the relevance of the material; quality is more important than quantity! Your portfolio should not consist of descriptive reports of your professional activities. You may include examples of personal reflective writing (not necessarily intended for publication) where they provide evidence of professional development.

3.4.2 Application form

When you are ready to submit your portfolio, contact the Qualifications and Professional Development Department (Email: *quals@cilip.org.uk*) to request an application form. This will enable CILIP to verify contact details and deal with any queries.

3.4.3 Portfolio presentation and submission

All portfolios should be

- written in the English or Welsh language
- divided into clearly marked sections as set out in the contents table
- word processed using a minimum of 12 point type size
- submitted in triplicate in separate binders, each bearing your name, membership number and current post

  or

  in triplicate on separate disks, in Word format. Each disk must be clearly marked with your name, membership number and current post

  or

  electronically. The first page should contain only your name, membership number and current post

- accompanied by an application form and the submission fee

If you are including in your evidence reference to words, ideas, structure or data by others, remember it is essential to acknowledge their contribution, through complete, accurate and specific citation.

3.5 Assessment

Once your application is received it will be sent out for assessment by members of the Chartership Board; the Board is appointed by CILIP Council (see Section 3.5.1).

Assessment will be carried out against the stated criteria (see Section 2) to ensure transparency and consistency of practice to all candidates. All applicants will be notified of

the outcome in writing within 10 working days of the date
of the Chartership Board Meeting.

3.5.1 Chartership Board

The Board normally has a total membership of 20. All are
Chartered Members or Fellows.The Board is appointed by
the Professional Development Committee of Council. A
number of those appointed have had experience of teaching
at postgraduate level and/or of examining at all levels
including research degrees. Meeting dates and the schedule
for sending in applications can be found on the CILIP
website.

Board members work in pairs when assessing applications
and these pairs are changed monthly. The allocation of
individual applications is undertaken by the Qualifications
and Professional Development Department. Confidentiality
is of prime importance to all aspects of the work of the
Chartership Board. No Board member will assess an
application submitted by a candidate who is known to them
personally or where the Board member feels their in-depth
knowledge of a workplace or organisation may inhibit their
impartial judgment of an application.

Candidates should note that the work of assessment is
carried on throughout the year but the formal ratification of
results can only be confirmed at a meeting of the
Chartership Board.

The Board is assisted in its work by a panel of Regional
Assessors, spread throughout the United Kingdom and
overseas. People appointed as Regional Assessors must have
been Chartered for at least three years. They will have either
some responsibility for (or strong interest in) professional
training and staff development, or expertise in a specific field
of library and information work. Regional Assessors are not

allowed to assess candidates who are known personally to them. It is the Board that decides what aspects of the candidate's application will form the basis of an interview with Regional Assessors, and this information is conveyed to both interviewers and the candidate by the Secretariat.

3.5.2 Assessment procedure

All applications are dealt with in strict rotation. Occasionally there may be queries that must be resolved before an application can proceed to assessment, for example if the minimum period of practical experience has not been met or if there is a query about membership.

The assessment of applications normally takes two to four months although, in some cases, as indicated above, it may take considerably longer.

3.5.3 Notification of results

If the Chartership Board is satisfied that your application meets the criteria for Chartered Membership you will be notified in writing and invited to join the professional Register. The date of admission to the Register will normally be that on which the Board accepts your application. Once admitted to the Register you may use the post-nominals MCLIP. You may continue to use them as long as you remain in membership of CILIP.

If the Board is not initially satisfied that your application adequately demonstrates suitability for Chartered Membership it may; ask for some sections of your portfolio to be re-written, request supplementary information or ask you to take part in a professional interview. In such cases you will be notified in writing of the additional requirements and given a time limit within which to submit or attend the interview.

The interview will normally be conducted by two Regional Assessors appointed by the Board. Topics for discussion will be notified to you. Under no circumstances will you be interviewed by anyone who knows you personally.

If your application is rejected you will receive feedback and comments from the Board and you will be able to re-apply. There is no limit to the number of applications you may make. The Board will confirm the earliest date at which you may re-apply. Further advice and guidance can be obtained from the Qualifications and Professional Development Department (Email: *quals@cilip.org.uk*).

3.6 Appeals

If your application is rejected you have the right to appeal according to procedures approved by Council. A copy of the Appeals procedure will be sent to unsuccessful candidates (see Section 4.2).

3.7 Continuing Professional Development

All Chartered Members are committed to updating their knowledge and skills and to improving their professional practice. This is clearly stated in the new *Ethical Principles and Code of Professional Practice for Library and Information Professionals*: www.cilip.org.uk/ professionalguidance/ethics.

Section 11 of the Ethical Principles refers to Members' "Commitment to maintaining and improving personal professional knowledge, skills and competences" and in the Code of Professional Practice – Section A: Personal Responsibilities it states:

"People who work in the information profession have personal responsibilities which go beyond those immediately implied by their contract with their employers or clients. Members should therefore:

1. strive to attain the highest personal standard of professional knowledge and competence

2. ensure they are competent in those branches of professional practice in which qualifications and/or experience entitle them to engage by keeping abreast of developments in their areas of expertise"

3.7.1 Revalidation

All Chartered Members are expected to participate in the voluntary Revalidation Scheme and to be assessed every three years. This will ensure that you have a formal record of your professional development. Full details of the Revalidation Scheme are in the Handbook available from the CILIP website: *www.cilip.org.uk/qualificationschartership*. You may also apply for Fellowship of CILIP after following two successful consecutive cycles of revalidation; further details of Fellowship may be obtained from the CILIP website at: *www.cilip.org.uk/qualificationschartership*.

4 Appendices

4.1 Royal Charter and Byelaws

The Royal Charter sets out the objectives of the Chartered Institute and provides the legal framework under which it operates. The Byelaws and the Regulations are an extension of this legal framework but are more flexible in that they can be changed from time to time. The Byelaws relating to the Register are available on the CILIP website: *www.cilip.org.uk/aboutcilip/howcilipworks/structure/ byelaws.htm.*

4.2 Regulations (2005 Regulations drawn up under Byelaw 11)

1. Registration

   All applicants for Chartered Membership will be required to complete registration forms and a Personal Professional Development Plan and send them to CILIP in order to register as candidates.

   All applicants applying for admission to the Register must:

   (i) Have been in membership of CILIP for a minimum of one year and be current members at the time that they submit an application for assessment

   (ii) Be Associate Members of CILIP

   (iii) Provide documentary evidence of meeting the admission requirements (see Regulation 2)

   (iv) Register for the CILIP Mentor Scheme or have been participants in another approved mentor programme

   (v) Have completed the required period of practical experience (see Regulation 2.1)

2. Admission Requirements

   You must have acceptable qualifications to be considered as a candidate for Chartered Membership. You will either have:

Pathway 1:

A Library and Information Studies qualification recognised or accredited by CILIP at Scottish Higher Education Level 10 or England, Wales and Northern Ireland Framework Level HE4 (or above).

OR you may have:

Pathway 2:

1. CILIP Certification (ACLIP) plus evidence of a minimum period of further personal professional development (see guidance notes)

   or

2. A CILIP accredited or approved qualification (an up-to-date list is available on the CILIP website at www.cilip.org.uk)

   (Holders of any qualifications listed under 2 will be required to submit copies of certificates etc. to CILIP for verification before registration can be confirmed)

2.1 Practical experience

All candidates must have completed a minimum period of appropriate practical work experience before submitting an application for assessment.

Pathway 1: One year full-time equivalent [FTE] work in a library and information service or related environment.

Pathway 2: Normally two years full-time equivalent [FTE] work in a library and information service or related environment.

[CILIP may authorise a reduction in the case of individual candidates who can demonstrate substantial

previous relevant practical experience, which could have been gained in another discipline]

For advice on the suitability of your work for eventual progression to Chartered status please contact the Qualifications and Professional Development Department (Email: *quals@cilip.org.uk*).

3 Application

3.1 Candidates will normally be expected to make an application for Chartered Membership within 1 year of completing the required period of practical experience.

3.2 Form of application

Each candidate will submit a portfolio including:

- Curriculum Vitae (CV).

- Personal Professional Development Plan (PPDP).

- Personal statement evaluating progress and achievements against the Personal Professional Development Plan (PPDP).The statement should be no more than 1000 words.

- Evidence of participation in a mentor scheme.

- Portfolio of supporting evidence.

3.3 Presentation

All applications must be in the English or Welsh language.

The documents should normally be word-processed or in electronic format and be accompanied by the appropriate form.

(Copies of certificates and other original documentary evidence may be sent by post, accompanied by a copy of your application form)

All applications should be accompanied by the appropriate fee, to be determined annually by CILIP AGM.

All documentation should be submitted to the Qualifications and Professional Development Department. All documents (electronic and hard copy) will be stored and treated in a confidential manner by CILIP.

4. Assessment

All applications are assessed by the CILIP Chartership Board that is appointed by CILIP Council.

Assessment will be carried out against clearly identified criteria to ensure transparency and consistency of practice to all candidates.

All applicants will be notified of the outcome in writing within 10 working days of the date of the Chartership Board meeting.

4.1 Criteria of assessment

All applications will be assessed against the same criteria. Candidates must demonstrate all of the following:

1. An ability to reflect critically on personal performance and to evaluate service performance

2. Active commitment to continuing professional development

3. An ability to analyse personal and professional development and progression with reference to experiential and developmental activities

4. Breadth of professional knowledge and understanding of the wider professional context

4.2 Forms of assessment

The Chartership Board will determine an appropriate method for the additional assessment of any application, where necessary, which may include one or more of the following:

(a) a request for additional written information and/or documentary evidence

(b) a professional interview of the candidate

4.3 Admission to the Register

The date of admission to the Register will normally be that on which the Board accepts the application.

Once admitted to the Register you must remain in membership of CILIP to retain the use of the post nominal letters MCLIP and to describe yourself as a Chartered Member.

5. Appeals

Candidates whose applications are rejected have a right of appeal according to procedures approved by Council. A copy of the Appeals procedures will be sent to unsuccessful candidates. (See Appendix 1 to these Regulations.)

6. Progression to Fellowship

Fellowship is the highest level of professional qualification awarded by CILIP. It is open to all Chartered Members who will normally have completed six years as a Chartered Member.

4.3 Appeals Procedure: Chartered Membership

1. An appeal may be made against a decision of the Chartership Board not to accept a candidate's Application for Chartered Membership submitted for the purpose of gaining admission to the Register.

2. A candidate whose submission is not accepted will be sent the following documents by Recorded Delivery:

    (a) A letter informing the candidate of the decision and the date of the Board meeting at which it was made.

    (b) Copies of the written reports of Board members setting out the reasons for rejection.

    (c) Copies of the reports of Regional Assessors if an interview was held.

    (d) A copy of this Appeals Procedure.

3. A candidate who wishes to appeal against the decision of the Board must do so within six weeks of the date of receipt of the Recorded Delivery letter referred to in 2. The Appeal must be made in writing to the Chief Executive, or to his/her Deputy.

4. The only grounds on which an Appeal may be made are:

    (a) That all or part of the information used by the Board was biased or incorrect due to no fault of the candidate and that the Board did not know this at the time it took its decision.

    (b) That the Board failed to follow its own published procedures and that this materially affected its decision.

5. The Chief Executive will decide whether there is a prima facie case for appeal. Where there is not he/she will inform the candidate of the reason for his/her ruling. In such cases there will be no further appeal.

6. Where there is a prima facie case for appeal, the Chief Executive will select a panel of three from up to twelve Chartered members, not members of the Chartership Board, chosen annually by Council from among its membership for this purpose.

7. The Chief Executive will set a date for the hearing of the Appeal to take place within six weeks of the date of receipt of the candidate's written Appeal.

8. The Chief Executive will send to each member appointed to the Appeal Panel a copy of the candidate's submission on his/her professional development, the papers sent to the candidate referred to in 2 above, and any papers sent by the candidate in support of his/her Appeal.

9. The candidate will be invited to attend the hearing of the Appeal and may be accompanied by a supporter. The Chair of the Chartership Board and the Head, Qualifications and Professional Development Department (or the nominee of either) should be present to represent the Board and its office based procedures. The Chief Executive should be present at all times to ensure that the Panel only consider matters appropriate to the Appeal and to offer advice.

10. At an Appeal Panel hearing the matters for consideration will be limited to:

    (a) Evidence from the candidate concerning the grounds for the Appeal, and details of how the information and/or procedures were faulty. The candidate should offer the correct information to the Panel. Panel members may question both the candidate and the representative of the Chartership Board. The Board representative should explain the reasons for any failure to comply with published procedures.

    (b) The candidate may ask the supporter to speak on matters concerning the grounds for the Appeal. The supporter may not assist (or speak for) the appellant in answering professional questions put by the Panel.

(c) The Panel will be concerned solely to test the candidate's claim that the Board used faulty information, biased statements or failed in its own procedures.

11. Where the Panel finds that the candidate's claim as set out in 10(c) has not been substantiated the Appeal must fail since the Board may not be challenged on other grounds.

12 Where the Panel finds that the candidate has made the case they will instruct the Board to review the matter. The Panel will give precise instructions to the Board as to the evidence which must be considered, and what must be discounted. The Chair of the Panel (with assistance from the Chief Executive) will detail the evidence accepted by the Panel. The evidence and decision cannot be challenged by the Board.

13. The Board will review the case at its next meeting after the Appeal Panel hearing. The Board will give written details of its decision to the Chief Executive and the Chair of the Professional Development Committee.

14. The Chief Executive will inform the candidate of the final decision of the Board.

15. All candidates are eligible to reapply. No candidate will have to wait longer than one year to reapply for Chartered Membership from the date of the original Board decision.

4.4 Open University Validation Service: Credit Accumulation and Transfer Scheme

The Open University Validation Service (OUVS) has agreed to award Masters level credits for successful completion of Chartered Membership and Fellowship.

The credit can be used in the OUVS Credit Accumulation and Transfer Scheme (CATS), and can be very beneficial to Chartered Members and Fellows who may wish to pursue a higher degree, as they can be used towards obtaining qualifications in a number of disciplines, not just library and information studies.

Full information, together with details of the specific academic general credit rating for both Chartered Membership and Fellowship can be found on the CILIP website: *www.cilip.org.uk/qualificationschartership*.

Further reading

Adair, J. and Thomas, N. (eds) (2002) *John Adair's 100 Greatest Ideas for Effective Leadership and Management*, Chichester: Capstone.

Adair, J. and Thomas, N. (eds) (2004) *The John Adair Handbook of Management and Leadership*, London: Thorgood.

American Association of Law Librarians (2001) *Competencies of Law Librarianship*, American Association of Law Librarians. Available at: *http://www .aallnet.org/prodev/competencies.asp* (accessed 28 December 2006).

Bee, F. and Bee, R. (1994) *Training Needs Analysis and Evaluation*, London: Chartered Institute of Personnel and Development.

Bee, R. and Bee, F. (1996) *Constructive Feedback*, London: Chartered Institute of Personnel and Development.

Belenky, M. F., Clinchy, B., Goldberger, N. and Tarule, J. (1986) *Women's Way of Knowing: The Development of Self, Voice and Mind*, New York: Basic Books.

Blanchard, K. and Muchnick, M. (2003) *The Leadership Pill: The Missing Ingredient in Motivating People Today*, New York: Simon and Schuster.

Blanchard, K. and Shula, D. (2002) *The Little Book of Coaching – Motivating People to Be Winners*, London: HarperCollins.

Blanchard, K. H., Oncken, W., and Burrows, H. (1989) *The One Minute Manager Meets The Monkey*, New York: Quill William Morrow.

Bodi, S. (1988) 'Critical thinking and bibliographic instruction: the relationship', *Journal of Academic Librarianship* 14(3): 150–3.

Boud, D., Keogh, R. and Walker, D. (eds) (1985) *Reflection: Turning Experience into Learning*, London: Kogan Page.

Bramley, P. (1996) *Evaluating Feedback*, London: Chartered Institute of Personnel and Development.

Bright, J. and Earl, J. (2001) *Brilliant CV: What Employers Want to See and How to Say It*, London: Prentice Hall.

Cane, S. (1996) *The Handbook of Skilful Management. A personal Programme to Develop Your Portfolio of Skills and Boost Your Employability*, London: Pitman Publishing.

Challis, M. (2000) 'AMEE Medical Education Guide No. 19: Personal development plans', *Medical Teacher* 22 (3): 225–236.

Chapman, A. (2006) 'Conscious competence learning model', available at: *www.businessballs.com/* (accessed 28 December 2006).

Cranton, P. (1992) *Working with Adult Learners*, Toronto: Wall and Emerson.

Eales-White, R. (1996) *How to Be a Better Teambuilder*, London: The Industrial Society/Kogan Page/Institute for Scientific Information.

Fisher, M. (1996) *Performance Appraisals*, London: Kogan Page.

Fletcher, C. (2004) *Appraisal and Feedback – Making Performance Work* (3rd edn), London: Chartered Institute of Personnel and Development.

Hardingham, A. (1995) *Working in Teams*, London: Institute of Personnel and Development.

Harrison, R. (1992) *Employee Development*, London: CIPD.

Hayden, P. (1995) *Learner's Pocketbook*, Alresford, Hampshire: Management Pocketbooks.

Heller, R. and Hindle, T. (1998) *Essential Manager's Manual*, London: Dorling Kindersley.

Henczel, S. (1996) 'Competencies for the 21st century information professional. Translating competencies into business competencies', available at: *http://www.sla.org/documents/conf/Competencies_for_the_21st.doc* (accessed 28 December 2006).

Honey, P. and Mumford, A. (1992) *The Manual of Learning Styles*, Maidenhead: Peter Honey Publications Ltd.

International Federation of Library Associations and Organisations (2000) 'Guidelines for professional library/information educational programs', available at: *http://www.ifla.org/VII/s23/bulletin/guidelines.htm* (accessed 28 December 2006).

Jackson, T. (2005) *The Perfect CV – How to Get The Job You Really Want*, London: Piatkus.

Kalinauckas, P. and King, H. (1994) *Coaching: Realising The Potential*, London: Chartered Institute of Personnel and Development.

Kearsley, G. (1996) *Andragogy*, Washington, DC: George Washington University.

Knowles, M. (1975) *Self-Directed Learning*, Chicago, IL: Follet.

Knowles, M. (1984) *Andragogy in Action*, San Francisco, CA: Jossey-Bass.

Kolb, D. (1984) *Experiential Learning*, Englewood Cliffs, NJ: Prentice Hall.

Kroehnert, G. (2004) *102 Extra Training Games*, Sydney: McGraw-Hill.

Lewis, G. (1996) *The Mentoring Manager. Strategies for Fostering Talent and Spreading Knowledge*, London: Institute of Management Foundation/Pitman Publishing.

Mackay, I. (1995) *Listening Skills* (2nd edn), London: Chartered Institute of Personnel and Development.

Mahmood, K. (2002) 'Competencies needed for future academic librarians in Pakistan', *Education for Information* 20: 27–42.

Marshall, J., Fisher, B., Moutlon, L. and Piccoli, R. (1996, revised 2003) 'Competencies for special librarians of the 21st century'. Submitted to the SLA Board of Directors by the Special Committee on Competencies for Special Librarians. Special Libraries Association, available at: *http://www.sla.org/content/SLA/professional/meaning/ competency.cfm* (accessed 28 December 2006).

McNeer, E. J. (1991) 'Learning theories and library instruction', *Journal of Academic Librarianship* 17(5): 2494–7.

McNeil, B. and Giesecke, J. (2001) 'Core competencies for libraries and library staff', in E. F. Avery, T. Dahlin and D. A. Carver (eds) *Staff Development: A Practical Guide*, Chicago: American Library Association; pp. 49–62.

Miller, J. Bligh, J., Stanley, I. and al Shehri, A. (1998) 'Motivation and continuation of professional development', *The British Journal of General Practice* 48 (432): 1429.

Mumford, A. (1995) *Effective Learning*, London: Chartered Institute of Personnel and Development.

Oncken, W., and Wass, D. (1974) 'Management time: Who's got the monkey?' *Harvard Business Review* 77(6): 75–80.

Race, P. and Smith, B. (1995) *500 Tips for Trainers*, London: Kogan Page.

Robbins, H. and Finley, M. (1997) *Why Teams Don't Work – What Went Wrong and How to Make it Better*, London: Orion Business Books.

Royal College of General Practitioners Working group on higher professional education. (1993) *Portfolio-based Learning in General Practice*. Occasional paper 63, London: Royal College of General Practitioners.

Russell, A. T., Comello, R. J. and Wright, D. L. (2006) 'Teaching strategies promoting active learning in healthcare education', *Journal of Education and Human Development* 1(1), available at: *http://www .scientificjournals.org/articles/1025.htm* (accessed 28 December 2006).

Smart, J. K. (2003) *Real Coaching and Feedback: How to Help People Improve their Performance*, London: Prentice Hall Business.

Stewart, D. M. (ed.) (1994) *Handbook of Management Skills* (2nd edn), Aldershot, Hampshire: Gower.

Stewart, J. (1993) *Speed Training: Systems for Learning in Times of Rapid Change*, London: BCA.

Stewart, J. (1996) *Managing Change through Training and Development* (2nd edn), London: Kogan Page.

Tamkin, P., Barber, L. and Hirsh, W. (1994) *Personal Development Plans: Case Studies of Practice, IES Report 280,* Brighton: Institute for Employment Studies.

Thorne, K. and Machray, A. (1998) *Training on a Shoestring*, London: Kogan Page.

Thorne, K. and Mackey, D. (1996) *Everything You Ever Needed to Know about Training*, London: Kogan Page.

Weaver, R. G. and Farrell, J. D. (1997) *Managers as Facilitators: A Practical Guide to Getting Work Done in a Changing Workplace*, San Francisco: Berrett-Koehler Publishers Inc.

Bibliography

Adair, J. (1997a) *Leadership Skills. Management Shapers*, London: Chartered Institute of Personnel and Development.

Adair, J. (1997b) *Leadership Skills. Training Extras*, London: Institute of Personnel and Development.

Bloom, B. J. (1956) *Taxonomy of Educational Objectives: Cognitive and Affective Domains*, New York: David McKay Company.

Boulter, N., Dalziel, M. and Hill, J. (1996) *People and Competencies: The Route to Competitive Advantage* (2nd edn), London: Kogan Page.

Cannon and Taylor Working Party Reports (1994) *Management Development to the Millennium*, London: Institute of Management.

Clutterbuck, D. (1991) *Everyone Needs a Mentor – Fostering Talent at Work* (2nd edn), London: Chartered Institute of Personnel and Development.

Gallway, T. (1975) *The Inner Game of Tennis*, London: Jonathan Cape.

Honey, P. and Mumford, A. (2006) *The Learning Styles Questionnaire 80-Item Version*, Maidenhead: Peter Honey Publications Ltd.

Knowles, M. (1984) *The Adult Learner: A Neglected Species* (3rd edn), Houston, TX: Gulf Publishing.

Megginson, D. and Whitaker, V. (1996) *Cultivating Self-Development*, London: Chartered Institute of Personnel and Development.

Parsloe, E. (1992) *Coaching, Mentoring and Assessing: A Practical Guide to Developing Confidence*, London: Kogan Page.

Parsloe, E. (1995) *The Manager as Coach and Mentor*, London: Chartered Institute of Personnel and Development.

Quality Assurance Agency for Higher Education (2004) *Publications: Progress Files for Higher Education*, Gloucester: QAA.

Special Libraries Association (2003) 'Competencies for the special librarians of 21st century' (revised edn), available at: *http://www.sla.org/content/SLA/professional/meaning/competency.cfm* (accessed 28 December 2006).

The Chambers Dictionary (1994) Edinburgh: Chambers Harrap Publisher Ltd.

Tuckman, B. W. (1965) 'Developmental sequence in small groups', *Psychological Bulletin* 63: 384–99.

Weightman, J. (1994) *Competencies in Action*, London: CIPD.

Whitmore, J. (1992) *Coaching for Performance: A Practical Guide to Growing Your Own Skills*, London: Nicholas Brealey Publishing.

Index